BEFORE YOU HIRE A YOUTH PASTOR

A STEP-BY-STEP GUIDE TO FINDING THE RIGHT FIT

MARK DEVRIES & JEFF DUNN-RANKIN

Before You Hire a Youth Pastor
A Step-by-Step Guide to Finding the Right Fit

group.com
simplyyouthministry.com

Credits
Author: Mark DeVries and Jeff Dunn-Rankin
Executive Developer: Nadim Najm
Chief Creative Officer: Joani Schultz
Copy Editor: Rob Cunningham
Cover Art and Production: Natalie Johnson and Riley Hall
Production Manager: DeAnne Lear

Library of Congress Cataloging-in-Publication Data

DeVries, Mark.
Before you hire a youth pastor : a step-by-step guide to finding the right fit / Mark DeVries and Jeff Dunn-Rankin.
p. cm.
ISBN 978-0-7644-7024-0 (pbk.)
1. Church youth workers--Selection and appointment. 2. Clergy--Appointment, call, and election. I. Dunn-Rankin, Jeff. II. Title.
BV4447.D4488 2011
254'.6--dc22
2011003656

ISBN 978-0-7644-7024-0

10 9 8 7 6 5 4 3 2 1 20 19 18 17 16 15 14 13 12 11

Printed in the United States of America.

"Hiring the right personnel is a fundamental responsibility of leadership. If you are in leadership at a church and looking to hire a youth worker, ***Before You Hire a Youth Pastor****, can save you a ton of heartache and time. DeVries and Dunn-Rankin know what they are talking about. This book will guide through a step-by-step, interviewing and hiring process critical to finding the right youth worker for your church. I couldn't recommend it more."*

—Dan Webster
Founder—Authentic Leadership, Inc.

---

*"****Before You Hire a Youth Pastor*** *should cause congregations to heave a collective, joyful sigh of relief: Finding a youth minister who 'fits' is not a mystery after all. Before you search—better yet, before you think about needing a search—put this book in the hands of every congregational decision-maker you can find. Too much is at stake not to."*

—Kenda Creasy Dean
Professor of Youth, Church and Culture, Princeton Theological Seminary
Author, *Almost Christian: What the Faith of Our Teenagers Is Telling the American Church* (Oxford 2010)

"Finding the right match for your church takes work and search teams need help. The authors of **Before You Hire a Youth Pastor** *believe, 'churches (not youth pastors) must own their student ministries and hire youth pastors who can steward those ministries for a season.' What a powerful insight! Brief, to the point, chapters provide practical guidance to search teams and contain more than 15 templates (Job Descriptions, Agenda for Search Team meetings, evaluating resumes, etc.), to help these teams. As a professor of youth ministry, I believe this book gives churches something it has needed for a long time: a systematic guide to making a discerning fit for your church. This book is a must read for a church seeking student ministry leadership."*

—Dr. Brian Richardson
The Basil Manly, Jr. Professor of Youth Ministry
The Southern Baptist Theological Seminary
Louisville, KY

DEDICATION

To Dad, for wisdom and opportunity.

To Mom, for vision and faith.

—Jeff

To Parish and Nealie, may the churches you grow up in help you love Jesus more because of what your Abu does.

—Mark

CONTENTS

BEFORE YOU READ: RECOGNIZING WHAT'S AT STAKE

INTRODUCTION

"GOOD MATCHES BETWEEN CONGREGATION AND PASTOR. THIS IS FAR MORE DEMANDING TODAY THAN IT WAS FIFTY YEARS AGO! THE DIFFERENCES AMONG GENERATIONS, AMONG INSTITUTIONS IN GENERAL...AND AMONG MEMBERS OF ANY ONE GENERATION...ARE FAR GREATER TODAY THAN THEY WERE IN THE 1950s. THE DEMAND TODAY IS FOR A CUSTOMIZED MATCH."

—LYLE SCHALLER, ***A MAINLINE TURNAROUND***[1]

You're searching again.

And if you're like most churches, it doesn't seem that long since you hired your last youth worker. And whether you are thrilled to have the chance to start over or grieving the loss of your most recent youth pastor or somewhere in between, we hope this little book can provide the introduction to the next chapter of your youth ministry. We hope to give you the tools you need to find the right staff person for your youth ministry as quickly as possible (but no quicker).

To get us started on the right path, we need to be clear about how this highly effective search process works:

- It isn't fast
- It isn't easy
- But it works

There are a few shortcuts, and rest assured that where they exist, we'll share them with you. But like the process of building a house, there are certain steps that must come *before* other steps—thus the name of our book.

We want to be very up-front here: A thorough search process results in hiring better-fit candidates. Better-fit candidates are likely to stay longer. And youth pastors who stay longer have a much greater chance of building a ministry that is sustainable beyond their tenure.

Ironically, churches that work the steps outlined in this book will need this book much less frequently.

But the opposite is true as well. Churches that rush the search process and hire quickly are less likely to hire well. Churches that don't hire well are more likely to see short-term, unhappy youth workers. A series of short-term, unhappy youth workers undeniably will have negative effects on the long-term stability of your youth ministry.

And so, we hope this little resource accelerates your search process by slowing it down, something that Fellowship Church just couldn't do.

THE FELLOWSHIP STORY

Fellowship Church was laser focused on hiring its next youth worker. When suggestions were made that the church first might want to do a little strategic thinking about the vision of the youth ministry, church leaders insisted that visioning would be the job of the new youth director.

The search had been going for nine months, built on the blind assumption that the person the church was looking for was just around the corner. In the meantime, the youth ministry was put on hold, the fabric of the youth ministry unraveled, volunteers scattered, and competing visions multiplied.

Finally, the long-anticipated day arrived. The new youth pastor took the reins amid great excitement and celebration. Within weeks of his launch, most of the volunteer team was happy to hand the responsibility over to him. They were exhausted, leaving him, as he described it, "a full year behind." That was the bad news.

The worse news was that the volunteers who did continue serving were motivated by an anxious desire to protect the competing corners of the ministry they had each shepherded for the past year—instead of eagerly embracing a new vision.

But after a year and a half of hard work, when the new youth worker was just beginning to get traction with his volunteer team and students, he got a call.

The camp he had grown up attending as a teenager, where he had served every summer during college, called to offer him the director's position. Although he loved his church, the new leaders he had recruited, the families, and especially the teenagers, this was a once-in-a-lifetime opportunity he simply couldn't pass up.

He left in the next month, and today the church is searching again, no further along than it was two years ago, destined to repeat the same cycle again, assuming that the smartest bet is to put all its eggs in the basket marked, "Just Hire the Right Youth Director…Fast."

This revolving-door approach to staffing a youth ministry has never worked very well. Here's why: When the youth ministry is built solely around the person in the role of youth pastor, you can count on a major disruption to your youth ministry every three years.

There is another way. And that's why we've written this book.

We are absolutely committed to seeing churches build sustainable youth ministries (see *Sustainable Youth Ministry*, InterVarsity Press, 2008) that last beyond the tenure of any given staff person. And to achieve this priority, we are convinced that *churches* (not youth pastors) must own their student ministries and hire youth pastors who can steward those ministries for a season. In the pages that follow, we'll provide you with a step-by-step process to begin making this shift.

WHO NEEDS THIS BOOK?

Maybe you're reading this book because you are a pastor who knows how crucial a successful youth pastor search will be for your entire church's future. Maybe you are reading this book because you have been hand-selected by your pastor to be the point person for your church's youth pastor search. Or maybe you're reading this book because you have just begun serving on a team of people charged with finding your church's next professional youth worker.

The biggest challenge you will face in your search process will not be finding the right people, or conducting the right interviews, or offering the right package. More than likely, the biggest challenge you will face is the chronic inexperience of the folks on your team. In our informal observations, most Search Teams are made up of people who have participated on an average of just over zero youth ministry searches. And as with the first time doing anything, the learning curve can be mighty steep. And so…

This is a book for **SEARCH TEAMS**: There are simply too many details related to an effective search for any single volunteer to reasonably manage all of them. For this reason, we have written this book primarily addressed to *teams* of volunteers charged with carrying out the details of the search process.

This is a book for **OTHERS IN THE CHURCH WHO NEED AN EXPECTATION ADJUSTMENT**: There may be a significant number of volunteers who do not serve on the formal Search Team but who will want to (and need to) have some investment in the search process. For example, the Search Team may solicit the help of a number of volunteers who will assist with making dozens of sourcing phone calls. It may be helpful for them to read this book, or parts of it, to understand the work they have been invited to do. There also may, at times, be members of the Youth Committee or Personnel Committee who can benefit from excerpts from the book to better understand the scope of the process and the anticipated timetable for hiring. A little book like this has the effect of getting everyone speaking the same language and working with the same informed expectations.

This is also a book for **SENIOR PASTORS**: In most churches, no one feels the pressure to hire well as much as the senior pastor does. Whether you as a senior pastor are leading the search yourself or delegating that task to others, it is likely that you simply don't have time personally to manage all the steps that need to be managed in a successful search. Of course, there are steps that only you can do, and we'll help you identify which those are, along with a clear step-by-step process for ensuring that all the other key details are completed.

YOU MIGHT BE ASKING...

Who are you guys?

We are youth pastors ourselves. Between us, there's over 50 years (and counting) of experience in the youth ministry world. And because we're old, we (almost weekly) hear from churches that are searching for youth pastors, and with about the same frequency, we hear horror stories of highly gifted youth workers who find themselves in impossible situations.

We have served on the lead staff of a consulting team called Youth Ministry Architects (ymarchitects.com) since 2002, providing coaching for pastors and youth pastors, assisting churches with youth pastor searches, and helping churches build healthy structures to maximize the chances of those youth pastors thriving in their roles.

Youth Ministry Architects frequently works with churches searching for new youth staff. Sometimes we get called just as a youth worker is leaving. Other times, churches call us when they wonder, after six months, if they have made the wrong hire. And still other times, churches want help moving strategically forward with a plan to adequately staff and support their youth ministry. But in every church we've served, building a healthy, well-equipped staff has been at the forefront of our work.

Are your stories true?

Well, sort of.

Based on our experience with 200 or so different churches, we've created composite stories, with new names and details. All the facts are true. We've just mixed them up to make them unrecognizable to any given church.

What is the difference between youth pastor, youth director, youth minister, and youth worker?

In different church circles, these terms can mean vastly different things. But in our little book, they all refer to the person your church will be hiring to fill a paid staff role in your youth ministry.

DON'T FORGET TO READ THE WARNING LABEL

If you sign on for the Search Team, you've signed on to do a good thing, and like most good things, it will at times be inconvenient and demanding, as well as deeply significant for the future of your church. As you read this book, probably over the space of a couple hours, you might feel overwhelmed by all the tasks before you. But you don't need to be. Remember: The tasks will be spread out over six months or so and will be shared by the good number of folks on your team.

Here's the way we think about it: If you were to sit down tonight and read all the recipes for your next six months of meals, that could feel mighty overwhelming. Consider reading this book the way you would a cookbook—skimming it at first and then just reading the chapters in depth once you get to that stage of the search.

Just remember that most shortcuts usually don't work. Though it may not feel like it now, **this resource *will* save you time**. We've provided you with more than 15 templates, guides, and scripts in the Appendix section (which are also available as customizable Microsoft Word® documents in the *Before You Hire a Youth Pastor Resource Pack*).

But the best way to save time in any search process is to spend a good bit of time on the front end getting all the right systems in place. Make no mistake about it. You might be able to complete your search more quickly by ignoring many of the steps we outline in this book. And there's a slim chance your gamble will pay off. But there's no guarantee.

Particularly if your church has had a lot of turnover in your youth staff (more than three youth directors in the past six years or long stretches without staff), you will want to stick closely to this process. With that level of turnover, there is likely something a little off-kilter in the systems surrounding the hiring, launching, and supporting of new youth staff. And this process will help tend to those things in ways that can vastly extend the longevity and effectiveness of your next youth worker.

Neither of us believes in gambling in youth ministry. We believe in investing. And smart investing requires a deliberate plan. If you want this search to be more than just another roll of the dice, this is the book for you.

Finally, we want to say thanks. You are about to invest your time in a process that has the potential to exponentially impact the teenagers in your church and community. You are about to bring sustainability to a process that can be very chaotic. And since you might not get a thank you note from your teenagers, we'll say it for them. Thank you for your time and your commitment. It will make a big difference in their lives—today, tomorrow, and well into the future.

BEFORE YOU START THE GAME: FIELDING YOUR A-TEAM

CHAPTER 1

> "COMING TOGETHER IS A BEGINNING. KEEPING TOGETHER IS PROGRESS. WORKING TOGETHER IS SUCCESS."
>
> —HENRY FORD

Not long ago, I (Mark) sat on a plane next to an assistant football coach from a major university. Ordinarily, I spend plane time working, but it was late. And since our flight had been delayed by a few hours, I fully intended to close my eyes as soon as we were in the air.

But when we touched down an hour or so later, I was still asking questions. This mountain of a man seated next to me was just returning from a recruiting trip, visiting high school sophomores and juniors. And because I am always fascinated to learn the processes leaders use to build great teams, I asked questions. Fortunately for me (and now for you), Coach was in the mood to talk.

As we talked across the empty seat between us, it wasn't long before he dropped a little rhyme into the conversation, speaking it as if I should have heard it hundreds of times before:

"Everybody talks about the Xs and the Os, but it all starts with the Jimmys and the Joes."

This highly successful coach, whose team you would immediately recognize, was laser focused on the first step of building a successful football program: not strategy but personnel—finding the right people, for the right positions, who fit with the right team.

And so it will be for you.

The first step—before looking at a single website or résumé—will be assembling the kind of team you will need for a successful search.

Though Coach shared an hour's worth of insights with me (many of which you'll find scattered through the pages of this book), all that counsel can be summarized in a single statement:

"If you're going to find and recruit great talent, it's going to take a lot of work."

In athletics at the college level and above, there are multiple full-time professionals trained in the fine art of scouting out great talent: researching backgrounds; interviewing teachers, coaches, and families; all the while listening between the lines for all that's not being said.

But in youth ministry, well...

We've observed it over and over again. Most churches approach the search for professional youth staff with no higher priority than this: Getting it done as quickly as possible.

We want you to get your search done as quickly as possible, but speed must never be the first priority.

That's why we've written this book.

In helping lots of churches over the years build a solid infrastructure for their youth ministries, often assisting in the hiring process, we've observed (and made!) plenty of unnecessary mistakes. Along the way, we've discovered a few nonnegotiable steps we hope you'll choose to take in your search process.

And so, like with any building project, it only makes sense to start with step one.

STEP 1: IDENTIFY A POINT PERSON FOR THE SEARCH TEAM

The Search Team will be the group that manages the entire search process. This team will meet regularly, report frequently to church leadership, and steward the process of hiring the church's next youth worker. And the point person for this team will be the one to ensure that the team stays on course.

Ordinarily the Search Team point person will work with the pastor to identify and recruit members of the team. He or she will be responsible for the successful launch of this process and, along with the senior pastor, will determine how to implement the steps outlined in this book.

STEP 2: ESTABLISH THE SEARCH TEAM

A solid search process does *not* begin with the search for the right candidate. It begins with the search for the right people to serve as a part of the Search Team. Though there may be many volunteers involved in the search who are not on the Search Team, it is important that this team include people who are willing and able to put in the necessary time. As a result, we recommend that the team be as small as possible but large enough to ensure that the load is not too overwhelming on any one person. A typical size for an effective Search Team is five to nine people (see Appendix A for a standard job description for the Search Team).

It will be important for those who agree to serve on this team to recognize that this will be a working team, *not an advice-giving team*. Important stakeholders in the youth ministry and church who only have time to give advice can be invited to provide input during the interview process, but those who serve on this team will be responsible for the load-bearing work of the search process. Each team member will be expected to take on weekly assignments that will move the search process deliberately forward.

STEP 3: ORIENT TEAM MEMBERS TO THEIR WORK

Once the team has been drafted, it will be time for the first "practice." In this first meeting, the team members will be introduced to the structure of the search process and will make a number of decisions about the ways they will work together, including:

- How often will the team meet?
- What roles will each member of the Search Team play? (See Step 8.)
- How will we engage support teams (see Step 8) in the search process?

- Who are the most important stakeholders to include on support teams?
- If necessary, determine what opportunities the Search Team will provide for appropriate people to process emotions related to the most recent youth staff departure. (See Step 7.)

BEFORE YOU SETTLE: PREPARING FOR AN *ABNORMAL* SEARCH

CHAPTER 2

["THE TYPICAL MISTAKE IS TO RUSH THE HIRING PROCESS, WHICH MEANS YOU'LL GET TO DO IT AGAIN SIX MONTHS AND FORTY THOUSAND DOLLARS FROM NOW."

—MIKE WOODRUFF, ***MANAGING YOUTH MINISTRY CHAOS***[2]]

When people ask for our most important piece of search advice, it all starts with two simple words: "Don't settle." Or pictured graphically:

The failure of the Johnson City United Church search was that they did just the opposite. They settled for a process that didn't require too much of the search committee. They settled for vague expectations for the work of the youth director. They settled for doing little or nothing to ensure that appropriate accountability structures would be in place to align their new youth director with the vision of the church. They settled for, well, being "normal."

Johnson City United Church simply conducted a normal search for a youth director—and they got predictably normal results. You are reading this book because you want your search to be *abnormal*. You want to avoid the wasted energy and money that are always bound up in a "normal" youth pastor search. And perhaps the best way to help you avoid a normal search is to provide a clear picture of what such a thing actually looks like.

STEP 4: UNDERSTAND THE TELLTALE SIGNS OF A "NORMAL" SEARCH

If you were like most kids growing up, you were ready to drive before you were *ready to drive*. You were likely impatient to get behind the wheel, impatient with taking the required drivers education classes, impatient with learning all the things you could do to avoid getting in an accident.

If right now, you are feeling similar emotions, we understand. But before your team actually gets behind the wheel, we want to make sure you know the eight traps we've seen a "normal" Search Team fall victim to:

1. **Hoping, wishing, and praying:** The normal youth pastor Search Team does little to prepare for or structure the search process. They post the opening, typically without a job description, a budget, or a timeline, repeating the comforting mantra, "How hard can it be?"

2. **Embracing "Superstar" mentality:** The normal Search Team works with the assumption that the new youth director can and should solve all of the problems related to the current youth ministry—and create no new ones! The Search Team members compliment themselves on "empowering" the new youth worker by not "saddling" him or her with any volunteers, planning teams, or calendars.

3. **Obsessing on the "Golden Age:"** Some searches are launched amid tremendous grief over the loss of the church's most recent youth director (or sometimes one or two youth directors back). The focus of the church becomes trying to find another Jimmy, another Melissa, another Jose.

4. **Stalling in terminal vagueness:** The normal church, to borrow from the language of *Sustainable Youth Ministry*, rushes out to hire "a dancer" before ever "building the dance floor" for the youth ministry. They assume that they serve the new youth pastor best by not providing any clarity about the desired direction for the program, when in reality the best candidates appreciate a clear

vision from the church. As a result, the youth minister at a "normal" church steps into his or her position with exactly zero measurable markers of what the church will view as effective ministry.

5. **Not preparing for the onset of weariness:** The normal Search Team is prepared for a sprint, not a marathon. The normal Search Team gathers a set of 10 or so résumés, has a few phone appointments, invites the top candidates in to interview, and then settles on hiring what will later be described as "the best of the weak candidates available."

6. **Failing to ask the hard questions:** A normal Search Team ignores the hard questions and, by doing so, dramatically increases the likelihood of unpleasant surprises early in the new youth worker's tenure. Hard questions include:

    - Have candid exit interviews been completed with youth staff members who have departed in the past five years, and have we identified what it was about the structure of their positions that may have caused them to leave when they did?

    - What kind of support structures will be in place for the new youth staff that weren't in place for our previous youth staff?

    - Do our expectations for the capacity and results of our youth ministry match the investment we are choosing to make in its success?

STEP 5: DEVELOP A SOURCING STRATEGY

Few aspects of a successful search are more often neglected than this one. And ironically, no single aspect of the search process will have nearly as profound an impact on the attitude of the Search Team as this one will.

Sourcing is, simply put, the process of talking to as many people as possible about the position, knowing that some percentage of those contacts will just happen to know someone (or know someone who knows someone) who might be a strong candidate for the open position. As strange as it may sound, sourcing is all about quantity, not quality. The ideal youth ministry search typically involves making a minimum of at least 200 sourcing contacts, though 500 would be far better!

Do the math with me: If team members talk to 100 possible sources, and 10 percent of them have a candidate to recommend (a fairly strong response rate), the result will be 10 potential candidates. By comparison, we like the churches we work with to have 20 to 50 decent candidates they have considered before starting the interviewing process.

Instead, the "normal" church starts interviewing with a small pool of candidates that no one is really all that excited about, often leaving Search Team members feeling desperate, wringing their hands, and complaining about how few strong candidates there are. This sense of desperation is often the primary reason churches choose to settle, rather than wait for the candidate who is an appropriate fit for the church's needs. We'd much prefer that you approach your decision making with the confidence that a big stack of good résumés can provide.

We know what you're asking next: "So where do we go to expand our list of sources?"

Your Search Team can choose from any of the following options. Use as many as you can:

- Publicly invite the entire church to submit names and contact information for anyone they know who might *either* be a strong candidate or someone who might know a strong candidate.
- Have everyone on the Search Team contact at least 10 friends who:
    - Are involved in the world of youth ministry in some other church
    - Are involved in ministry of some kind
    - Are in churches that have strong youth ministries
    - Have a strong connection with a Christian camp or college
- Ask each of the members of the church staff for recommendations of possible sources that the Search Team should be talking to.

- Contact the church's denomination or association headquarters for the names and contact information of potential sources. (A great question would be, "Who are 10 people in our denomination that are doing great youth ministry these days?")
- Depending on the ideal age of the candidate you are seeking, you may want to contact all colleges that provide a youth ministry major to ask for their recommendations.
- If you are searching for a candidate with a seminary degree, you will want to contact feeder seminaries for churches like yours.
- Contact Christian camps within your general area (or around the country) for names of people who have served as counselors in recent years who might be searching for a youth ministry position.
- Have everyone on the Search Team scan online for *names* in youth ministry that seem to occur over and over again, and contact those people for recommendations.

In addition, we recommend that every Search Team select at least 10 "sourcers" who aren't on the Search Team but might be willing to make 10 contacts of their own.

At this point in the process, the Search Team will want to determine its sourcing strategy and set a target number of sources that the team and its recruits will talk to before actually starting the interview process.

You can get a jump start by assigning someone the job of checking with some of our favorite sources—the online job banks at SimplyYouthMinistryTools.com/jobs, YouthSpecialties.com, YMArchitects.com, and HireAYouthPastor.com.

STEP 6: CRAFT YOUR TEAM'S "ELEVATOR SPEECH"

Now that your team has spent many hours building the foundation for your search, you are ready to create what we call your "elevator speech. "This is the brief explanation of your church, the kind of person you are searching for, and the unique opportunities in your particular church. As the name suggests, this is a pitch short enough to give during a short elevator ride—about 20 seconds.

A good elevator speech keeps your team on the same page and ensures constancy in the messages that are being given to sources, candidates, and references. You will want to write it down and share it with the whole team, with your "sourcers," and in conversation with all the candidates your interview.

Unfortunately, most teams' elevator speeches sounds something like this:

We are a great church in a wonderful city! We have tremendous youth in need of a committed person who can lead our youth ministry.

Compare that elevator speech to this:

First Church is willing to invest in youth ministry. Having just doubled the size of our youth staff, we are seeking a highly creative high school director to focus primarily on our weekly outreach program to youth outside our church walls. Because we have a diverse staff, this person will be relatively free from logistical details and will be able to focus primarily on relationships.

Or this:

We are a theologically conservative church with a progressive worship style in search of an ordained youth pastor to lead our active and committed group of volunteers. The focus of our youth ministry is discipling students who will, in turn, impact their friends and families. We already have most of the key volunteers in place.

STEP 7: IDENTIFY UNFINISHED BUSINESS FROM THE MOST RECENT YOUTH STAFF DEPARTURE

It is a rare search that has no residual concerns related to the departure of the most recent youth worker. It is normal for students, parents, and leaders to feel a wide range of often conflicting emotions—grief, fear, anger, sadness, relief. The normal church provides very little opportunity for processing these emotions in healthy ways; as a result, those emotions go underground, often surfacing in sabotaging ways for the next youth director.

It is for this reason that the abnormal Search Team will want to consider, as a part of its process, creating a space for listening and gathering input from students, parents, and leaders who simply need a place to process all they are feeling related to the current transition. This processing could take place in a town hall meeting, in focus groups, or in one-on-one meetings with those who may have deep-seated emotions related to the previous youth pastor, the processes surrounding his or her departure, and the future of the youth ministry. In each setting it will be important for the team to provide a relaxed setting for listening, especially for those who might have felt the most deeply wounded. This will also be the place for the team to transparently communicate how the search process will take place.

BEYOND "ONE MORE TIME—THE WAY IT'S NEVER WORKED BEFORE"

Leaders at Epiphany Church had done all the normal things. They had posted the job at local colleges. They had scoured the Internet. They prayed and hoped and worried. Nearly a year later, they had a handful of OK résumés, none of which had them dancing in the aisles.

They refused to settle, though, and during this season of waiting, they set some three-year goals and built a great team of volunteer leaders. They also hired a part-time person they called "the organized mom" who made sure the ministry kept moving—that vans were rented and events were publicized. In month 10 of the search, just as everyone was growing weary, the Search Team agreed to reboot the search process and go back to sourcing again (something they had done halfheartedly months earlier). Team members all agreed to "call a dozen contacts, no matter how far-fetched, just to see what happens."

Jean called a friend at her old church, hundreds of miles away, and said, "Who do you know?" That's how they found Molly. She was the daughter of a friend of a friend, working part time at a small church, and she was ready for the next step in her ministry. Molly turned out to be the perfect fit for Epiphany, and five years later, she is still there. So are the "organized mom" and almost the entire group of fantastic volunteers.

If your church chooses to run an abnormal search for a youth pastor, there's a very good chance you'll experience abnormal results. You may just have a youth worker who stays more than the disappointingly normal minimal tenure. You may just hire a youth pastor who is able to hit the ground running rather than spending the first year plowing new ground.

You may just hear a steady drumbeat of teenagers and families and youth leaders aligned and moving powerfully in the same direction.

Our hope for your church is that this search experience lays the groundwork for a deliberate process that can be used again and again. The *abnormal* church doesn't simply search; it builds a sustainable search process.

Ironically, the churches that use this process (and have it in place for future searches) are the very same churches that tend to need it the least.

Now, let's get to work.

BEFORE YOU LAUNCH: STRUCTURING YOUR TEAM

CHAPTER 3

"YOU START BY FOCUSING ON THE FIRST WHO PRINCIPLE—DO WHATEVER YOU CAN TO GET THE RIGHT PEOPLE ON THE BUS, THE WRONG PEOPLE OFF THE BUS, AND THE RIGHT PEOPLE INTO THE RIGHT SEATS."

—JIM COLLINS, ***GOOD TO GREAT AND THE SOCIAL SECTORS***[3]

Christ Community Church's leaders had run a normal, everyday, garden-variety search for a youth pastor. When all was said and done, it was not nearly as hard as they expected—just a couple meetings and a few phone calls here and there. In fact, after they collected seven résumés and gave the best three to the senior pastor, he talked to all three candidates and picked a favorite that week. They brought Kirk in for a visit two weeks later.

He wasn't outstanding—at first glance, he had a little swagger and he only did a so-so job of connecting with parents—but the students loved him, and he was certainly the best of the bunch. Plus, he was ready to start. The whole thing was over in a record eight weeks, and the Search Team members complimented themselves on their speed, because after all, the youth deserved to have a youth pastor as quickly as possible.

Three months later, they fired Kirk.

He had undeniable skills with teenagers. What he didn't have was the ability (or much interest) to do more than "hang out" with the eight or so that he felt comfortable with. Parents wanted to support the youth ministry, but they felt like they were always out of the loop. And when they asked Kirk for more regular information, Kirk would say impatiently, "All they need to do is check the website!" When the pastor began to press

Kirk for more accountability in his contact work, Kirk dug in his heels and said, "I love my boss, but he just doesn't understand youth ministry."

After Kirk and the church parted company, the Search Team re-formed. This time, Amy, who had a daughter in the youth program, volunteered to be part of the team. Amy was head of the human resources department of a large insurance company, and she'd been down this road before. She wasn't the chair of the committee, but she showed team members how to use their network of contacts to gather 40 résumés instead of seven. She encouraged them to add a few key positions on the team, including one of the church's great hostesses who took on the role of making candidates feel great about their on-site visit. Another member used his bookkeeping skills to help them do a better job of tracking where the candidates were in the system.

At the end of this much-improved process, they hired Tammy, who was a much better fit for Christ Community Church. She is still there after six years. This search took longer, and it was a lot of work. But the work was shared by people in specific roles that they were well-equipped to play. The results made the big investment worth it.

STEP 8: AGREE ON THE STRUCTURE OF THE SEARCH TEAM

Like an athletic team, an effective Search Team works best when each member knows his or her position and plays it faithfully. Though some responsibilities will belong to everyone on the team, the search process can run much more smoothly when a few key roles are assigned at the outset.

Like the actors in a community theater troupe, some of your players will take on more than one role. The key is to make sure from the outset that each role is assigned to someone on the team. You'll want to avoid the common mistake of loading the moderator with the majority of the responsibilities, a mistake that invariably creates a bottleneck in the process.

The Moderator (or Search Team Point Person): Ideally, the moderator of the Search Team will have read this book before moderating the orientation meeting, preparing him or her to answer any questions that new team members might have about this process. The moderator will be responsible for preparing the agenda for each meeting and, ordinarily, for maintaining strong communication with appropriate staff, leaders, and committees in the church.

The Task Manager: Most teams have a "secretary" who takes notes at each meeting. Our experience, though, is that these notes are seldom ever looked at again. We recommend that a Search Team, instead, appoint a task manager. The task manager will end every meeting with a reminder of what each person has agreed to do before the next meeting and will begin every meeting by asking for a progress report from each team member related to his or her assigned tasks.

The Sourcing Coordinator: The typical search will require a team to make personal contact with *at least* 200 possible sources. Because engaging a broad range of sources is so crucial to the effectiveness of the search process, you will want someone in this position who can mobilize not only the Search Team but also a variety of other stakeholders in the church to tap into their own networks. Our experience is that few things impact the quality of a candidate pool quite like connecting with people who connect with people who might know someone who knows someone who might be just the candidate your church is looking for.

The Candidate Tracker: This person will take responsibility for tracking every potential candidate, those who have submitted résumés, as well as those candidates who may not be looking but whom the Search Team has decided to pursue. This tracking would include keeping a record of any contacts made by team members and when the contacts took place, along with results and next steps. This person will also send quick notes, ordinarily via e-mail, to candidates to let them know their résumés have been received and whether they are still in the running.

The Reference Check Tsar: This person will assign reference check phone calls and background research assignments to members of the Search Team and perhaps to additional search support volunteers. This research would include less formal methods of gaining information on potential candidates, like researching those candidates' blogs, Twitter® messages, websites, and online social networking sites like Facebook®. The reference check tsar will record and track the results of all reference checks and background research, typically only for "top five" candidates.

The Phone and Video Interview Coordinator: Once the team has developed a list of top five finalists, the phone interview coordinator will coordinate the assignments of individual phone interviews for the Search Team. These screening interviews will generally be less than 30 minutes, with each interviewer using a standard set of interview questions. (See Appendix I for an outline of the interview process and a menu of phone interview questions.) The phone interview coordinator will maintain a record of interview notes for each finalist and make arrangements for video interviews for any finalists remaining after the initial phone interviews, including scheduling with the candidates, arranging for appropriate technology, and other similar tasks.

The On-Site Interview Manager: When it is time to bring candidates in for on-site interviews, it will be helpful for someone on the Search Team to be responsible for all logistics: booking flights and hotels (as appropriate), drafting interview schedules, coordinating the schedules of various staff and stakeholders involved in the interview process, and inviting appropriate people to the various stages of the interviews. This person would also arrange for someone to host each candidate during his or her visit.

The Communications Meister: This person will make sure that regular, appropriate updates on the search process are given to the staff, youth leaders, parents, and the congregation as a whole. These updates could come in the form of newsletter articles, requests for prayer in the worship bulletin, "minutes for mission" in the church's worship services, website articles, and visits to staff and leadership meetings. When the new youth staff person is hired, the communications meister would draft the letter to go out to the congregation and/or youth families.

The Database Manager: This person will take responsibility for ensuring that accurate contact information is collected and readily available for all members of the team, including:

- A directory of all members of the Search Team
- A directory of all other stakeholders who will be participating in the search process in some way
- A directory of potential sources and a record of which team members contacted them and the result of the contact

STEP 9: FIELD YOUR TEAM

In addition to those serving on the Search Team, there are also a number of roles for other people willing to assist in the search process:

- **"Sourcers"** are individuals recruited to make at least 10 phone calls or e-mail inquiries to friends and business contacts in search of people who might know someone who might be a fit for the open position. These are typically church members who are not serving on the Search Team. In a standard search, we look for 20 or so sourcers (see Appendix E for a standard job description for sourcers).

- **Pastors and Staff** will almost always be involved in the search and hiring process. Since each pastor will have different ways that he or she might choose to be involved, the Search Team's moderator will meet with the pastor(s) and staff to gain clarity on their desired involvement. In addition, the senior pastor (or in some cases the executive pastor) will provide the best counsel for which teams and/or committees in the church will need to be involved in the process—and when that involvement should occur.

- A variety of **Church Committees and Teams** will need to be brought into the loop at various points in the process. Since churches vary widely in their structure, it will be the job of the Search Team to gain clarity about each committee or team's appropriate role, typically asking the following questions of the following teams:

  The Personnel Committee

  - Does anyone from the Personnel Committee need to be involved in the interview process?

  - Is there a liaison from the Personnel Committee who will need regular updates from the Search Team?

  - What steps will the Personnel Committee require before the next youth staff member is hired?

The Finance Committee

- What is the budget for hiring the next youth staff member?
- What is the budget for the search process? (A good rule of thumb is one to two months of the youth director's salary. That should cover any advertising, travel and lodging, meals, and welcome parties.)
- At any point in the process, does the Finance Committee expect communication from the Search Team?

The Youth Ministry Committee or Youth Leadership Team

- When do members of these teams need to be involved in the process?
- Do any of these leaders expect to have input into the hiring decision?

The Church Council, Vestry, Session, or Elder Board

- What expectations about the search are there from the group of leaders charged with oversight of the entire church's ministry?
- Will these leaders expect to interview the candidate, simply receive a report from the Search Team, or something in between?

- **Interviewers** may be added to the search process when candidates are interviewed via videoconferencing or brought in for on-site interviews. For example, it might be important for every candidate to meet for an interview with a few parents, volunteer leaders, or students who are not a part of the Search Team.
- **The Follow-Up Specialist(s)** can make sure that everyone who submits a résumé receives prompt communication from the church and that everyone who interviews receives timely follow-up as well. Though this position could be folded into a member of the Search Team, our experience is that members of the Search Team quickly become overloaded with responsibilities, making candidate follow-up their most frequently dropped responsibility.

- Select **Students** will need to be involved in the process at some level. It will be the role of the Search Team to decide the specific roles students should play and in what settings. Though churches vary widely in their approach to this question, the most common placement of students in the search process is as advisers to the process, called on for input at specific decision-making points.

- **Consultants** have increasingly become the choice of churches that wish to shorten the learning curve and broaden their capacity for an effective search. Consultants can share in sourcing, posting, developing timelines, training the Search Team, or managing the entire search process. Ordinarily, funding for a consultant can be made available painlessly by accessing the money budgeted for the hire of the still-unhired new youth worker. If you are already at the point in this book that you feel like all this attention to structure is more than your team can reasonably pull off alone, you may want to consider a consultant.

Once the Search Team is in place, that group will determine which of the above teams will be needed and in what ways.

WE KNOW...

We just shared a mighty long list with you. You might be tempted to peg us as overachievers and scratch a few of those players off your roster. We certainly did that same thing ourselves in the early days. But here's what we learned:

- It will likely cost more time that it saves.

- The poor moderator will discover that all those jobs really do need to be done, so he or she will try to stuff another dozen duties into an already overflowing task bucket.

- It will communicate to the most desirable candidates that this is a church that simply doesn't know what it is doing.

- The likelihood of hiring the wrong person multiplies exponentially, which can be costly in more ways than dollars.

- And most importantly, your ministry to teenagers will likely suffer as a result.

Not getting a team in place before starting the search process is like starting to play a football game with only half your players. It may save time in the short run and make the spectators happy, but it's no way to win the game. After cleaning up more than a few youth ministries whose churches tried to shorten or ignore the "Field your team" step, we were compelled to offer something better.

BEFORE YOU HIRE THE DANCER: BUILDING THE DANCE FLOOR

CHAPTER 4

"THE FUNDAMENTAL TASK OF LEADERS IS TO DEVELOP CONFIDENCE IN *ADVANCE* OF VICTORY, IN ORDER TO ATTRACT THE INVESTMENTS THAT MAKE VICTORY POSSIBLE—MONEY, TALENT, SUPPORT, LOYALTY, ATTENTION, EFFORT, OR PEOPLE'S BEST THINKING."

—ROSABETH MOSS KANTER, *CONFIDENCE*[4] (EMPHASIS ADDED)

Fran had a deep commitment to young people, an undeniable love for Christ, and a willingness to learn. The church had an undeniable willingness to invest sacrificially in youth ministry.

How could such a perfect combination possibly go so wrong so quickly?

Franklin Road Community Church leaders called us after their youth director announced her resignation after less than two years. Her hire had come amid a passionate funding frenzy, fueled by statements like this:

- *If this church really cared about kids, we'd find the money!*
- *It's time for us to put our money where our mouth is!*
- *We are losing our kids, and we're trying to build this program with nickels and dimes!*

And so, frenzy won the day. This small-town, small church put its money where its mouth was, creating a salary package for the new youth pastor significantly higher than any other staff person at the church, other than the senior pastor. The leaders of Franklin Road Community Church were sure that if they simply put enough money into a full-time youth worker, they could turn the tide of inconsistency that their church had experienced in its youth program for over two decades.

After a long and arduous search, the church hired Fran, a young woman in her early 20s with minimal youth ministry experience and a degree in physics. When progress came more slowly than expected, it wasn't long before people began to talk: "Did you know that Al, clearly the best associate pastor we've ever had, is making less than that new youth director, even though he's been here for 15 years?" And before long, the pressure on the youth pastor to produce immediate, visible results intensified greatly.

The new youth director inherited almost zero infrastructure for the youth ministry. What she did inherit was an intense backbiting battle between the two strongest volunteers on her team. Results were going to be very slow in coming.

Caught trying to please two particularly vocal, anxious, and angry volunteers, Fran could feel herself being squeezed into a no-win situation. It wasn't long before the anxiousness and anger turned against her, and the financial frenzy reversed its direction:

- *This kid [the youth pastor] gets paid more than 75 percent of the people in our church make, and what does she do all day?*
- *I heard that Al [the popular associate pastor] was thinking of leaving our church because he's so frustrated with the way he's been treated...I would be, too!*
- *It's been six months. How could one person accomplish so little in six months! What are we paying her all this money for?*

And much too soon after Fran was hired, she had begun looking for another position. The unrealistic expectations and the acidic climate between the volunteers left Fran questioning her own competency and call.

Though FRCC missed a number of steps in their search, its leaders' fundamental mistake was failing to make an informed decision about what sort of staff they actually needed. They assumed that hiring a full-time, high-dollar youth worker from out of town was the only possible option, for no more logical reason than the fact that the bigger churches in town staffed their youth ministries that way.

But there just might have been another way.

STEP 10: CLARIFY THE SYSTEM THAT WILL SURROUND YOUR NEW YOUTH PASTOR

When launching a youth ministry search, it is easy for the Search Team to forget that its primary purpose is *not* to hire the church's next youth pastor. This principle is so easy to forget that we want to say it loudly to every Search Team: **YOUR MOST IMPORTANT JOB IS *NOT* TO FIND YOUR CHURCH'S NEXT YOUTH PASTOR.**

It will be marvelous if the church hires a great youth director quickly. **But the larger purpose of this search is to help the church build a great youth ministry.** And believe it or not, those two priorities are not always the same.

We've seen churches hire exceptional staff in their youth ministries, only to see those youth directors (and those youth ministries) flounder for years. These ministries didn't fail because of a lack of desire, a lack of investment, or a lack of effort. They almost always failed because the staffing design was simply not a match for the church's needs or expectations.

A few examples:

- One church hired a single staff person to run a program that had more than 200 active youth involved.
- Another church hired an ordained staff person who had "grown out of sleeping on gym floors" and expected him to have the same magnetism as the 25-year-old who had just left.
- Another church hired a stable of three interns with no one to train, guide, and supervise them.
- Still another church hired the highly relational, creative, "outrageous" 25-year-old who described himself as an administraphobe (self-defined as "someone with an irrational fear of administrative work") as the sole staff person for a ministry involving 50 to 100 youth.

> "YOUR MINISTRY IS PERFECTLY DESIGNED TO ACHIEVE THE RESULTS YOU ARE CURRENTLY GETTING."
>
> — ANDY STANLEY, REGGIE JOINER, AND LANE JONES, *SEVEN PRACTICES OF EFFECTIVE MINISTRY*

We do believe that finding great staff is key to developing a thriving youth ministry. But superstar success in one place doesn't always transfer to the new environment. Just look at the track record of the NFL's top draft picks. Not so great.

The smarter plan is to focus on what we can control over the long haul. We need to take responsibility for creating systems and processes that will allow an above-average person to deliver exceptional results.

Without the appropriate infrastructure, even the most gifted youth pastors have little chance of success. Most long-term, thriving youth ministries we've seen are led by a team, not by solo superstars. Of course, we've seen *inflated* youth ministries lead by solo superstars. But as soon as that superstar leaves, the wind immediately goes out of the sails and the ministry stalls dead in the water.

The book *Sustainable Youth Ministry* recommends that every church consider building a staff that includes three different roles:

The Architect: This *person* (it almost never works when this role is assigned to a committee) midwifes the church's vision for its youth ministry and designs systems and structures to help the church achieve its vision. This role is the one most often ignored in churches, resulting in youth ministries that run frantically before ever deciding where they are going.

The Construction Foreman: This person coordinates the flow of work to be completed by a wide variety of laborers who share in the building process. This person doesn't *do* the work but makes sure that all the workers are in the places they need to be, with the materials they need to have, at the time they need to be there. This is the second most neglected position, resulting in youth ministries that have no shortage of good ideas and well-meaning people but whose work never successfully moves forward.

The Laborer(s): These are people with specific skills for ministry—programming, relationships, event coordination. The typical church hires a person extraordinarily gifted in a single aspect of ministry (building relationships with students, for example) and then expects that person to play all the other roles required for building a thriving youth ministry. This approach is no more effective than hiring an electrician to build an entire house. Frustration, guesswork, and incomplete projects are the most common results of this approach to hiring.

How can your team determine the appropriate staff configuration for your unique setting? To help answer that question, we've put together a little multiple-choice survey that can be found in Appendix B. The survey provides only sustainable options. In other words, if you don't find the option your team is planning to take, there's a good chance that your "successful" search (getting somebody hired) will not move your church a single step forward toward building an effective ministry.

Just for fun, we've included a supplementary survey in the *Before You Hire a Youth Pastor Resource Pack* that includes the most common *non-sustainable* ways that churches choose to answer these questions.

STEP 11: CONSIDER ALTERNATIVE MODELS

The most common model for staffing a youth ministry is to hire a solo practitioner and hope for the best. Though we've seen this model work in some settings, it is the approach taken by a gambler, not an investor. After a decade, the typical church using this model has had an inconsistent series of short-tenured staff, each with a vision for ministry different than the one before, each leaving the ministry no further along than when he or she began.

Before you take a gambler's route, we want to invite you to consider a number of investor's options. You may settle on the solo-practitioner model, but you will do so with eyes wide-open and an awareness of the structures you'll need to have in place to maximize your chances of your next youth pastor actually moving your youth ministry forward.

We are fully aware that many of our readers might be thinking, "Wait a minute. I thought we were the youth pastor Search Team. Do you mean we might not be looking for a youth pastor after all?"

If it feels like a step backward, it should.

The foundational question of your staffing model is something we urge you to step back and consider before you start the heavy lifting of your search. We urge you to get crystal clear about where you are going before you start running.

To help Search Teams in their discernment process, we've developed a straightforward filtering process, a series of yes/no questions you will want to answer to put a fine point on exactly what you will be looking for in your next youth staff person.

1. **Could we accomplish the results we are looking for with a part-time person, rather than a full-time person?**
   If your church would be thrilled to have a ministry that involved 25 youth or less, our opinion is that, at least at this point, you don't need a full-time youth worker. The most effective model we have seen for sustaining ministries of 25 or less is to hire someone from inside the church to work 20 hours a week or so to manage the youth ministry as the "general contractor."

   We have seen quite a few churches sustain strong and healthy ministries with this model. But before buying into this approach, your team should be warned: This is not a job for a highly anxious, reactive, defensive parent who takes on the job because he or she has never been satisfied with the youth ministry. This person must bring a spirit of non-anxious playfulness to this work, as well as being organized (or creative) enough to juggle the many facets of the youth ministry.

2. **Do we hire from within our church?**
   Hiring from within brings a number of advantages:

   - **Stability** (this person is not likely to cycle out of the ministry after a few years)
   - **Relational capital** (this person is already known and trusted by the potential volunteers and parents in the congregation)

- **Coordination clarity** (the congregation, parents, and students will not expect this person to be a pied piper but to coordinate systems that will build momentum for the ministry and excitement among the students)

Many churches choose to avoid hiring from within out of fear of the potential ripple effect of things not working out. Surprisingly, our experience is that there is very little difference between the negative ripple effects of a person hired from within or from outside the church. Both will require crystal clear expectations from the outset, including agreed-upon systems of accountability.

3. **Do we want to hire interns?**
Interns will, no doubt, be the least expensive option for hiring youth staff, and for good reason. They are called "interns" because they are, by definition, in need of significant coaching and mentoring. Any church that chooses to hire interns must have a "general contractor" in place who can not only help the interns grow spiritually but who can define clear expectations and accountability systems for these young leaders, most of whom are in their first "real job."

   One effective model we have seen is a part-time youth program coordinator (general contractor) who manages the logistics of the ministry, including the supervision and development of a part-time intern or two who bring relational energy and youthful creativity to the program.

4. **Do we want to hire an ordained pastor to oversee our youth ministry?**
Here's a pattern we've seen frequently:

   A church hires a highly relational "teenager magnet" who can't organize his way out of a paper bag. When this youth staffer leaves, there is a pendulum swing in the next hire, as people say:

   - *"We need someone with some maturity!"*

- *"If this church really cared about teenagers, they would hire a pastor to work with them, not just an entry-level person who comes to make all their mistakes on us!"*
- *"We can't afford not to have a senior person in this position!"*

The "put-your-money-where-your-mouth-is" frenzy wins the day. The church hires a "mature" associate pastor, assigns him or her a pile of general pastoral responsibilities, and is surprised when he or she does no better than the much cheaper youth worker who was just replaced.

I am an ordained pastor, and for the past 20+ years, I have worked with students week in and week out at my church (so I obviously think having pastors involved with youth is important). But when I served as the solo staff person in our ministry (for the first five years or so), we stayed stuck, only getting traction when our ministry was the kind of staff constellation we have described above.

5. **How long do we expect our next youth staff person to stay?** A church communicates its expectations of longevity by its salary package. With the exception of churches that hire from within, a church that is expecting a two- or three-year commitment should offer a starting salary in the 20s or low 30s. A church hoping for a three to five-year commitment should be starting in the 30s to low 40s. And for a church hoping to land a youth pastor who will stay six years or more, it would be logical to start at least in the 40s or low 50s. Of course these numbers can vary greatly in different parts of the country and are representative of normal minimums at the time of this writing.

   The one exception to this rule is if you hope to be a church that "grows its own superstar." Your church may want to invest in professional coaching and mentoring for a young leader who has the potential to stay for a long time, starting him or her at a lower-than-normal salary with the understanding that with intentional coaching, his or her learning curve could be significantly shortened.

6. **Is this job complex enough to require outside help?**
Some churches determine, after seeing the complexity of building a sustainable ministry in their particular context, that the least expensive, highest leverage investment they can make is to partner with a consulting group that specializes in playing the "architect" role. Consultants can offer a strategic design to be implemented by the rest of the staff, as well as providing coaching and alignment work with the new staff when they arrive.

STRUCTURE MATTERS

Coastal Christian Church was a large church with great people on its youth staff. But for years, its youth ministry had the reputation as being the church's most glaring weakness. But today, CCC's youth ministry is seen as its shining star, one of the church's greatest reasons to celebrate. What changed?

- It wasn't the staff themselves. The lead youth staff members stayed the same.
- It wasn't the amount of time they invested. The lead staff continued to spend almost exactly the same amount of time they did before their realignment.

What did change was the alignment of their positions from an accidental to a deliberate, sustainable structure. Whether you choose to go the way of Coastal Christian by bringing in outside help or you choose to sort out these questions internally, don't turn the page without making sure your team has addressed the fundamental structure questions of this chapter.

BEFORE YOU POST: AGREEING ON YOUR SEARCH TIMELINE

CHAPTER 5

> "YOUTH MINISTRY IS VERY DIFFICULT WORK, FAR MORE DIFFICULT THAN PARENTS AND CONGREGATIONAL LEADERS REALIZE. THE PRESSURES ON A YOUTH MINISTER ARE ENORMOUS, AND THESE PRESSURES ARE ONES FOR WHICH FEW HAVE BEEN ADEQUATELY PREPARED."
>
> —MERTON STROMMEN, ET AL, *YOUTH MINISTRY THAT TRANSFORMS*[5]

The first thing eager Search Teams tend to do is to start posting their job openings in as many places as possible. Eager searching senior pastors start calling their friends to dig up any leads they can.

Of course, networking and sourcing *are* important steps. But when these are disconnected from a deliberate search process, these efforts are little more than shots in the dark, evidence again of a gambler's mindset, not an investor's.

An effective Search Team recognizes that no single step is nearly as important as the step of building the system itself.

Like in any building project, certain steps must come in order. A builder could…

- Run the wiring for a building *after* hanging the drywall; it will just take 10 times as long to achieve the same result.
- Lay the foundation after having framed and roofed the house, but the required extra efforts would be herculean.
- Start the plumbing after laying the floor, but not without endless backtracking.

We have discovered a tool that keeps the many steps in order: a deliberate, no-nonsense timeline.

A timeline maximizes the possibility of a search that is short as possible, while still being effective. A timeline represents a starting point, a project management plan that can be expanded, contracted, or adjusted for the unexpected (which should only be expected). Our experience tells us that a timeline with a six-month horizon tends to be a reasonable starting point.

With absolute certainty, we know that the speed of an *effective* search hinges on how well the initial, foundational steps are completed. Skim over these steps and you can easily find yourself doubling back, doubling your work, and finding yourself more stuck six months down the road than you were when you first started.

STEP 12: AGREE ON A TIMELINE FOR YOUR SEARCH

Though this book provides you with all the steps you will need to complete your search effectively, you will still need to create a timeline that for your unique context. We've provided a resource insert in the *Before You Hire a Youth Pastor Resource Pack* that takes the 37 steps found in these 10 chapters and puts them in a format that can allow your team to put target dates next to each step or outcome, as well as the name of the person who will take responsibility for each step. The following template will give you some idea of the items you will find in the timeline in that additional resource.

Month 1: Laying the Foundation

- ☐ Begin recruiting the Search Team
- ☐ Select a team leader
- ☐ Agree on a date for the Search Team orientation
- ☐ Read *Before You Hire a Youth Pastor* (at least to the point of this timeline) to understand the scope of the search process
- ☐ Orient the Search Team (See Chapters 1-2)
- ☐ Customize the Search Timeline (this document)

- ☐ Agree on the systems that will surround the new youth staff person
- ☐ Agree on alternative models for staffing (See Chapter 4)
- ☐ Confirm the job description(s)
- ☐ Agree on list of posting locations; Appendix F lists a few of our favorites, but there are more

Month 2: Posting, Sourcing, and Collecting Résumés

- ☐ Request input and approval from the appropriate leaders in the church for job description and job posting
- ☐ Make posting assignments and begin posting
- ☐ Create automatic response processes for résumés that are received
- ☐ Distribute sourcing assignments
- ☐ Begin sourcing
- ☐ Define the church's vision for its youth ministry in writing
- ☐ Draft articles to be placed in the church newsletter and website to update the church family on the search
- ☐ Continue sourcing
- ☐ Collect at least 25 résumés

Month 3: Background Research, Phone and Video Interviews

- ☐ Continue sourcing
- ☐ Collect at least 40 résumés
- ☐ Identify the top five candidates selected
- ☐ Make reference check assignments for the top five candidates
- ☐ Make background research assignments for the top five candidates

- ☐ Make screening interview assignments for the top five candidates
- ☐ Assign Search Team "host" to each of the top five candidates
- ☐ Schedule and complete videoconference interviews for the top three to five candidates
- ☐ Background research and reference check information gathered for top candidates
- ☐ Decision made about doing another round of phone interviews before face-to-face interviews (with the same or different candidates)

Month 4: Finalist Interviews

- ☐ Face-to-face interviews scheduled and completed with top two or three candidates

Month 5: Offer Making

- ☐ Offer made and accepted (or the search process rebooted)

Month 6: New Staff Orientation and Welcome

As you can tell, a six-month timeline for a search is very aggressive, often dependent on best-case scenarios, with all the right pieces falling into place at just the right time. Unfortunately, best-case scenarios are predictably rare, so your Search Team will want to make a timeline that is realistic for your particular context. Churches that want to speed the process can telescope all the steps outlined between Month 1/Day 14 through Month 2/Day 14 and accomplish the vast majority of those steps in a five- or six-hour orientation retreat.

STEP 13: DRAFT THE JOB DESCRIPTION(S)

As strange as it may sound, the vast majority of youth workers we speak with indicate that they do not even *have* written job descriptions, and those who do usually can't find them! And as a result, most are evaluated (and evaluate themselves) by vague notions of "success," often informed more by a secular business mindset than by a biblical framework for faithful ministry.

Your starting point should be to discover whether the church has a standard format for its job descriptions. If it does, you will want to build your job description using that format. If not, we recommend creating the job description around results (for example, "40 youth are involved on an average Sunday morning") rather than activities (for example, "attends staff meeting weekly"). For an example of a results-based job description, see Appendix C.

Once the job description is drafted, you'll want to gather input from the pastor(s), the Personnel Committee, and any other stakeholders who might need to be consulted before the job description becomes official.

STEP 14: MAKE SURE YOUR CHURCH HAS A CLEAR, EXPLICIT, WRITTEN VISION FOR ITS YOUTH MINISTRY

We know. Conventional wisdom suggests that the Search Team must *wait* for its new youth pastor's arrival before worrying about the vision for the youth ministry. This assumption is built on the very unsustainable idea that it is somehow the new youth worker's job to tell the church what ITS vision for youth ministry should be.

Ignoring the task of bringing some clarity of vision into the search conversation is a mistake for all kinds of reasons:

- If the youth worker stays the average youth worker tenure, you'll be looking for the next youth pastor to bring *another* brand-new vision for youth ministry again in less than four years.
- The pastor and church leadership already have expectations for the youth ministry. When those expectations are not clearly spelled out, you can expect unnecessary conflict and often the premature departure of your newly hired youth worker.
- The vision for youth ministry in any given church belongs to the church leadership, not to a series of youth pastors.
- It is the youth pastor's job to steward *the church's* vision for youth ministry, not the other way around.
- Churches that actually have a vision for their youth ministries almost always have longer tenured youth staff than they would have if no vision were in place.

Though it is outside the area of direct responsibility for the Search Team to *develop* a vision for the church's youth ministry, your team can play a crucial role in working with the church leadership to catalyze the process for clarifying this vision. If there is no process or vision in place, the Search Team will want to meet with the senior pastor and any other key stakeholders in the youth ministry to develop a "top 10" or "top five" list that can be used to provide the new youth worker with at least a starting point of unambiguous markers of success, as defined by the church leadership.

STEP 15: BEGIN TO COMPILE KEY SEARCH DOCUMENTS

By this point in your team's work, you will have looked at lots of different sheets of paper in different Search Team meetings. Now is the time in the process to compile these key documents in a way that can keep all the members of your team on the same page. You will likely already have

- a contact directory for everyone on the Search Team
- a contact directory (organized by roles) of any additional people who will be involved or assisting with the search in some way
- the job description for the desired position
- any visioning documents that are in place for the youth ministry (even if those visioning documents are simply a set of key bullet points collected by the Search Team)
- the search timeline
- the posting descriptions

At this point, you will also want to create and/or compile

- any visioning documents the church might have (for the entire church)
- a spreadsheet that will allow you to track which candidates are in which category (such as top tier, possible, dropped)
- a spreadsheet for tracking all sourcing assignments

STEP 16: BUILD THE AUTOMATIC RESPONSE PROCESS

As you begin the process of receiving résumés, your team will want to ensure that "automatic response processes" are in place. This simply means that your team has made sure, before receiving the first résumé, that each person who inquires, interviews, or sends a résumé will receive an appropriate response.

The simplest process we have discovered is for your "candidate tracker" to respond to every résumé as soon as it arrives—typically by e-mail. A short, cordial form letter is sufficient, thanking each person for the résumé and explaining that you will be narrowing the field to your top five by a particular date.

The candidate tracker can include on the master candidate list the date a note was sent to each candidate. The candidates who are sweating it out at home will appreciate this simple practice. And as a bonus, it will make your position more attractive than 90 percent of the other churches' Search Teams, distinguishing your church as one that cares deeply about youth ministry.

Your candidate tracker will want to e-mail a candidate tracking summary to the Search Team prior to each meeting, a habit that builds a helpful accountability factor into the process (for a sample candidate tracking summary form, see Appendix G).

IF YOU BUILD IT...

I have always been fascinated by the final parable of the Sermon on the Mount in Matthew 7. I am struck by the fact that both builders exerted exactly the same amount of energy, but only one house remained standing.

A successful search is not dependent on your highly anxious efforts and hard work. It is dependent on ensuring that before the first walls go up, a foundation is in place that can withstand the worst-case-scenario realities.

BEFORE YOU PHONE: PREPARING FOR PHONE INTERVIEWS

CHAPTER 6

> "LONG-TERM THINKING IMPROVES SHORT-TERM DECISION-MAKING."
>
> —BRIAN TRACY, *EAT THAT FROG*[6]

"I guess now we just start calling?" Stan wondered aloud as the Search Team meeting was getting under way. He looked at the pile of 30 résumés in despair. "This is crazy. How in the world are we supposed to pick our next youth pastor from...*this*?"

"I know," said Lynn, the single mother who had reluctantly signed on to the Search Team, unable to say no to the senior pastor. With her head swimming, she affirmed Stan's sentiment. "Last night, I looked through résumé after résumé, and they all started to run together. I don't think we're any further along than we were eight weeks ago!"

Jen, the team leader who had been through this process before, interrupted the spiral: "I don't know. As far as I can tell, we're right on schedule. It's just time to take the next step."

Jen understood what most Search Teams forget at some point in the process: It is absolutely normal—especially at this point in the process—to feel overwhelmed and off-course.

Of all the searches we've been involved in, there hasn't been a single one that didn't hit a snag at some point in the process. When (not if) your team hits a point of frustration in your search, there's a very good chance that you are "right on schedule."

The only way for the team to move beyond its debilitating sense of aimlessness is to continue deliberately working the process. A team overwhelmed by how far the finish line feels can most easily be re-energized by only one thing: taking the very next step.

STEP 17: PICK THE TOP FIVE

Once your team has received 20 résumés or so, it will be time to identify your top five candidates in your current pile. If your résumé pile is thin, you might need to simply take another two weeks to repeat Step 5, beating the bushes just a little more to increase your pool of candidates.

We admit that there is a certain level of uncertainty at this stage of the process. A piece of paper can never convey a person's total personality, fit, and gifts for ministry, but this "rough cut," based only on résumés, will help to narrow the field. Rather than identifying each candidate as a "yes" or a "no," we recommend at this point in the process that you place each résumé in one of the following three categories:

- **Category 1:** The "Want to Pursue" pile will include the candidates whom you think could be a great fit for your ministry, based on

    - their résumés
    - a strong recommendation
    - or some X factor that particularly appeals to you (like skill in leading worship or a connection to your alma mater)

  It's OK at this point to have a few questions about them, questions like

    - "Is she overqualified?"
    - "Why was he only at his second job for 10 months?"

  You can always dig deeper during the interviews.

- **Category 2:** The "I Doubt It" pile will include those, for whatever reason, you see little likelihood of succeeding in this particular position. These may be candidates who have a theological perspective or denominational background inconsistent with your church or whose education or experience level would not be appropriate for your position. This pile might contain full-time students who couldn't possibly handle a full-time ministry job or people whose résumés give you a negative gut instinct.

If some on your team are queasy about putting anyone in the "I Doubt It" pile, remember that this process is not about judging the worth of a particular candidate as a human being; it is about identifying their fit for your church's particular needs.

- **Category 3:** Once you have created the first two categories, every other résumé will belong in the "Maybe" pile.

Typically, you'll want to wind up with four to six people in the "Want to Pursue" pile. If you have fewer than four, your team can decide either to add in a couple more from the "Maybe" group or just go after your top three. If you have more than six, you'll want to come to some consensus about which candidates to pursue first. It will be helpful to remember that you can always go back to the "Maybe" pile if your first rough cut doesn't produce the caliber of candidates you are looking for. You can also spend some more time beating the bushes and making contacts.

STEP 18: ASSIGN A POINT PERSON FOR EACH FINALIST

Once the team has narrowed the finalist list to five or so candidates, each of the finalists will be assigned to one of the members of the Search Team. Every team member assigned a finalist will serve as the point of contact for that candidate, complete a screening phone interview in the next seven days, and recommend that the candidate move either to the video interview stage or be moved to the "I Doubt It" pile or the "Maybe" pile.

The person on the Search Team responsible for coordinating phone interviews (see Chapter 3, Step 8) will be responsible for helping the team stay on track with its initial screening phone interviews.

The "Phone Interview Coordinator" will

1. assign each finalist to a member of the Search Team
2. distribute the standardized interview questions (see Appendix I)

3. track the completion of phone interviews

4. compile notes from each of the completed phone interviews

These short phone interviews—described in greater detail in the next chapter—will give the team enough data to determine whether or not it will be worth the time of the entire Search Team to interview this candidate together via video. A simple way for phone interviewers to make this recommendation really boils down to the answers to three straightforward questions:

1. Does he or she fit our job description?

2. Does he or she fit our church?

3. Do I like this person?

Because the youth minister position is all about developing relationships, you'll want to ask yourself how comfortable you personally are in conversation with this candidate. If you don't get off the phone saying, "Man, I really enjoyed that phone call," then you might want to move this candidate out of the finalist pile and into the "maybe" pile.

BEFORE YOU INVITE: SCREENING AND RESEARCHING YOUR TOP CANDIDATES

CHAPTER 7

["MEASURE TWICE, CUT ONCE."

—LESSON LEARNED ON YOUTH MISSION TRIPS]

The résumé was flawless and impressive. The Search Team members were unanimous in their enthusiasm that Hank was unquestionably a candidate to bring in for an interview. Though the team members were tempted to call immediately to coordinate a date for a visit, they resolved to stick to the process and do a little background research first.

And that's when I got the call from my friend in Michigan, who just happened to be a member of the Search Team. She had noticed that Hank was currently serving a church in my hometown. And knowing how connected the world of youth ministry can be, she called to see if I knew anything about him. Knowing her church well, I was eager to do anything I could to help my friend with a successful search.

I let her know that Hank's résumé wasn't lying. He was *great* at his job; parents and kids loved him. I raised two concerns: He had only been in his current position for three years, and, theologically, he and the Michigan church were at totally opposite ends of the spectrum. He could undeniably lead their youth ministry but not likely in the same direction that the pastor and church leaders were going.

As much as I hated to say it and as much as my friend hated to hear it, it would not be fair to Hank or to the church to try to force a match just because Hank was great at youth ministry and the church was needy. The likely result of calling Hank to this church would be an explosion of popularity for the youth ministry, followed by a sharp division between

Hank and the church leadership, likely followed by the acrimonious departure of Hank (and a few angry families).

We've watched church after church put incredible effort into organizing elaborate face-to-face interviews for candidates with whom they have become infatuated. In the process, they often avoid doing the kind of background research that will ensure that those visits will be consistently productive.

This story is not simply a reminder that impressiveness in a candidate is not enough. In this case, the story is a reminder of the power of completing a screening process for a candidate from many different vantage points. If there is one step we've seen churches skip (to their own peril) more frequently than any other, it is this one.

This chapter outlines how to maximize standard screening processes as well as tapping into a variety of nontraditional ways of learning about your top candidates before going to the expense of bringing them in.

STEP 19: CONDUCT SHORT SCREENING PHONE INTERVIEWS

Once you have narrowed your search to the top five, you'll be ready to conduct your first screening interviews by phone. This is not the time for a full interview but simply a 15- to 30-minute conversation, usually with a single member of the Search Team, designed to determine if there are any reasons not to move forward with reference checking and scheduling a video interview with the entire Search Team.

The screening interviewers would seek to accomplish five things:

- Quickly schedule a phone interview
- Conduct a phone interview using the standardized interview questions agreed on by the Search Team
- Summarize the notes from each interview in one page or less
- Send those notes to the phone interview coordinator by the agreed-upon deadline
- Recommend to the Search Team whether or not to move to scheduling a video interview with this candidate

The purpose of the call is to

1. identify any glaring red flags that might prevent this candidate from being a good fit for your church.
2. present the candidate with an honest, compelling picture of your church and the position.
3. gain information about alternative sources of getting to know this candidate.
4. gain enough information from the candidate to make an informed recommendation about whether he or she should remain in the top five.

STEP 20: MAKE REFERENCE CALLS

Once a member of your team has completed a screening call and made the recommendation that a particular candidate remain on the finalist list, it will be time to make reference calls.

When your team makes reference calls, you may, very infrequently, come across a surprise, like "No, Bobby never actually worked here." But most references will speak in exclusively positive terms about the candidate.

The key will be to leave every reference call with a little more clarity about the candidate's unique strengths, weaknesses, and fit for your position. Remember the rule: People (especially in youth ministry) tend to do what they like to do and tend to do well where they have done well in the past, regardless of what their job descriptions say they should be doing.

So one way to get the most out of your reference calls is to listen for the "sweet spot" of the candidate you are calling about and determine how close it is to the most important priorities of your youth pastor position.

Two examples might be helpful:

- Morristown Community Church hired a youth pastor who, in her previous position, just didn't have time to work hands-on with students, ostensibly because of the extraordinary amount of administrative requirements. In interviews she expressed great enthusiasm about actually having time available to be with students in this new position.

But once on the scene, although most administrative duties were taken off her plate, it quickly became clear that building friendships with students outside of youth meetings just wasn't something she felt comfortable doing. A good reference call should reveal those things that a particular candidate actually IS doing, not simply those things he or she aspires to do.

- St. Stephen's had been burned by its last superstar youth director, who built an inflated ministry almost entirely around himself, and when he left, so did the church's youth ministry. So in this search, the church was committed to building a strong volunteer team.

  When Jimmy interviewed, everyone was blown away by his energy and creativity. When they asked how he felt about building a team of volunteers, he responded with his typical enthusiasm: "You just can't build an effective youth ministry without a strong volunteer team. Though my circumstances didn't allow me to build one in my old church, I would be totally committed to it here."

  But within a year of his arrival, despite the fact that he had extensive relationships with students (just like he'd had at his previous church), the volunteer team was anemic at best, with most of the previous volunteers having resigned since Jimmy's arrival.

In both these scenarios, a solid reference-checking process could have prevented the youth ministry from hiring someone with great gifts but not the gifts needed to move the particular church's youth ministry forward.

Here's how you can set up the reference-check process for your search:

The reference check tsar should take responsibility for assigning reference check calls and background research projects to members of the Search Team and perhaps to additional search support volunteers. He or she will also record and track the results of all reference checks and background research for all the finalists.

The team members will need to decide if they want to assign the task of reference and background checking only to members of the Search Team or to other youth ministry stakeholders who were not able to serve on the Search Team. Because reference checks routinely take longer than expected, make sure that those doing the calls are willing to begin the process immediately, ideally turning in their information to the reference check tsar within one week of the assignment.

It will be important for the callers to know that the reference-check process will likely require that they make multiple calls in the week because many references do not immediately (or ever) call back following a first message. Reference callers should plan on 15 to 30 minutes for each reference called.

Appendix L provides a handy guide to help those making reference calls with this filtering process.

STEP 21: GATHER ALTERNATIVE BACKGROUND INFORMATION

In addition to the traditional reference-checking process, there are a number of ways of learning (sometimes more accurate) information about your top candidates before bringing them in for a face-to-face interview. The gathering of alternative input on your top candidates can be done by someone on the Search Team, by the person doing the reference checking, or by someone assigned specifically for this role (like a highly invested student who is great at navigating social networking sites).

Contact non-listed references: If the candidate's list of references does not include anyone from a pertinent season in his or her life (for example, a church where the candidate served for nine months), be sure to do a little digging in that area. Ask the candidate for permission to call that church or business as part of your normal reference-checking process. When following up with these sources, be sure to ask that key question: "Would you rehire this person? Why or why not?"

E-mail a short reference questionnaire: You can increase the number of references and reduce the amount of time required by taking advantage of the Internet. You can create a short questionnaire and ask your top five candidates to forward that questionnaire to their references. The references then e-mail their answers directly to the Search Team.

This can increase the number of references who respond because it is the candidate who is doing the inviting. We have included a sample reference questionnaire for e-mailing in the *Before You Hire a Youth Pastor Resource Pack*.

Conduct a criminal background check: Before you invite a candidate on site, you will want to run the criminal background check. You can save a few dollars by only doing this for the person you are about to offer a job, but most human resources managers can tell you an embarrassing story about announcing a job offer to the rest of the company ("But only if he passes the background check—ha ha"), then having to quietly rescind the job offer. Your church probably has a process in place that you can use.

Check your own personal network: Someone recently sent me an e-mail asking about a candidate who was applying for a position 500 miles away from where I live. "I don't suppose you know him," they wrote, taking a stab in the dark.

No, but I knew a lot about the church he worked at and the success of their programs. I also knew someone who used to work with the candidate. A quick phone call provided the Search Team with very helpful information to pass along. So ask yourself whether anyone on your committee or in your church might have a personal connection. Do they know someone in the candidate's hometown or at the summer camp where the candidate worked last summer? Does your pastor know someone at one of the churches on the résumé?

Leverage the power of the Internet: You can be pretty sure the candidate used the Internet to research your church. The question is whether you want to do the same tool.

Though there are ethical issues involved in taking advantage of Internet search engines and social networking sites like Facebook®, most of those concerns can be resolved simply by asking for the candidate's permission to learn more about him or her through his or her Facebook®, blog, or website. There is also a good possibility that you can simply use Google® to search your candidate's name along with the term "youth ministry," and you'll likely get dozens (if not thousands!) of results.

Some people see these Internet tools as extremely helpful in a search, capable of revealing things that the candidate might not bring up in an interview. Others see them as the equivalent of poking around through someone's garbage can in the middle of the night to see what dirt you can find. Your team will want to have a discussion about using the Internet to research your top candidates, and check with your church's attorney to ensure that you are in compliance with the latest laws related to what information you can and cannot use.

STEP 22: PREPARE FOR THE VIDEO INTERVIEWS

Once the list of finalists has been confirmed after the screening interviews, it will be time to schedule video interviews with the entire Search Team. The number of finalists will likely be less than the number of those screened.

When possible, it is helpful to have several interviews scheduled an hour apart on the same day. A tech-savvy member of your congregation or staff can show you how to use complete videoconference calls over the Internet. Vendors like Skype® allow anyone to turn almost any computer into a videoconference-call machine. All you'll need is a computer with a microphone, audio capabilities, and a built-in camera. Some Search Teams have had success attaching their computer to a LCD projector, giving the entire group greater access to the candidate on video.

Whether your team uses a projector or simply gathers around one table with a computer screen in the center, you will want to decide ahead of time what the protocol will be: Who will moderate? What is the procedure for interjecting follow-up questions?

Using the sample questions from Appendix M as a starting point, the Search Team will want to agree on a set of no more than 10 questions that will be asked. Here are a few of our favorites:

- We know you enjoy all kinds of teenagers, or you wouldn't be in this business. But what kind of students do you enjoy working with the most?
- What are the parts of a normal youth ministry job that you would give away if you could?
- Tell us about something that happened in your past youth ministry experience that really energized you.

- Tell us about something that happened in your past youth ministry experience that deflated your energy.

What questions do you have for us? (Be prepared to answer with "I don't know, but I'll find out.")

STEP 23: CONDUCT THE VIDEO INTERVIEW

As you begin this exciting phase of the search, here are some things to remember, to help you maximize your short 45-60 minutes with each candidate.

1. **Be prepared to let the person talk**

   Seek to find some common ground, to put the candidates at ease, to communicate that you like them. But you'll want to avoid helping them tell their stories. Do not interrupt them or coach them or hint at the "right" answer. Allow them to talk, even if it means some periods of awkward silence.

2. **Remember: The candidate isn't the only one being interviewed**

   The person you are calling has a decision to make, too, and is probably looking at more than one church. At this point, you are this candidate's first picture of the personality of the church. Fortunately, you were probably selected for the Search Team because you are just the kind of person that great youth ministers want to come work with. Just be aware that you're on stage, too.

   Early in the conversation, you'll want to include the elevator speech about the position (see Step 6 in Chapter 2), including what you particularly love about your church and its youth ministry and why you're excited about the opportunity for the next youth pastor. Just make sure you're description is accurate, which leads us to…

3. **Tell the truth even if it hurts**

   Unfortunately, the old joke, "How can you tell a search committee is lying?" (Answer: "Their lips are moving") is too often true. Sometimes, search committees, in their eagerness to woo "the right" candidate will shade the truth about their church. Here are a few of the most common search committee white lies:

What is said: *We don't care about numbers.*
What is meant: *...unless you don't produce them.*

What is said: *We just want you to bring your own vision for youth ministry and implement it here.*
What is meant: *...unless it doesn't work.*

What is said: *This church is willing to do whatever it takes to build a top-flight youth ministry.*
What is meant: *...unless it involves hiring more staff or increasing the size of the youth budget.*

Giving prospective candidates information you wish were true will not help them or your future ministry. In fact, when interviewing staff for our own youth ministry, we often start by telling them all the reasons someone *wouldn't* want to work here. After 10 years or so of this kind of interviewing, not a single candidate has been scared away by the honesty. And our staff has been able to enter into the challenges of youth ministry with eyes wide-open to the immense expectations that will be placed on them.

4. **Ask yourself: "Does this person fit the job description?"**

The general rule is that in a job with as much flexibility as youth ministry, the youth pastor will end up doing most what he or she enjoys doing—no matter what the job description says. You'll want to ask about a few of the key priorities on the job description to discover if the candidate has any successful history doing similar things. Listen for what stories the candidate tells with excitement and evaluate how those passions fit the job description.

5. **Ask yourself: "Does this person fit the church?"**

Youth ministers (like the rest of us) tend to flourish where they're not fighting the system, and teenagers are best served when parents and the youth minister have shared values and vision. It may not always be important to have someone from your denomination serving as your youth pastor, but the person you hire will need to be in the same theological ballpark as your church. A candidate who laces his language with buzzwords like "getting saved" may not be a great fit for highly liturgical Episcopal church. And likewise, a candidate who speaks of the "justice and love of the triune God" may not be a fit for a highly informal evangelical church. Remember, you are not making a judgment on the theological correctness of these candidates as much as you are discerning a fit with your unique context.

6. **Ask questions that lead somewhere**

   In addition to the basic questions you will find in Appendix M, you may also want to ask about questions raised by the candidate's résumé. For example:

   - Why such a short tenure at the last church?
   - What's the story on the one-year gap in your employment history?
   - What has led to you feeling called to youth ministry after two decades in retail work?
   - I notice there are no references from your last church. Is there someone there we could talk to about your experience there?

   It may also be helpful to request alternative ways of getting to know the candidate. You can ask permission to "friend" the candidate on Facebook® or to follow that person's Twitter® or blogs.

IN SUMMARY...

After this multistage screening process, your team should have plenty of information to determine whether it is time to schedule an on-site visit or time to move the candidate back to the "Maybe" list.

BEFORE THE ON-SITE INTERVIEW: MAKING PLANS TO MAKE A GREAT FIRST IMPRESSION

CHAPTER 8

> "FIRST CHURCH IS LOOKING FOR THE BEST STAFF POSSIBLE. MAKES SENSE, RIGHT? THIS REALITY IS CLEARLY STATED BY THE LEADERS INVOLVED IN THE SEARCH FOR NEW STAFF. THE GOAL IS TO ASSEMBLE AN ALL-STAR TYPE STAFF, THE BEST AVAILABLE IN EACH ROLE. THE ASSUMPTION IS THAT THIS WILL MAKE THE GREATEST IMPACT ON THE CHURCH AND THE COMMUNITY. THE ASSUMPTION HAS THE APPEARANCE OF WISDOM BUT IS FAULTY.
>
> "IT HAS PROVEN FAULTY FOR FIRST CHURCH. THEIR PRESENT STAFF IS FULL OF GIFTED PEOPLE, BUT THEY ARE RUNNING IN DIFFERENT DIRECTIONS."
>
> —THOM RAINER AND ERIC GEIGER, ***SIMPLE CHURCH***[7]

Everybody loved Jimmy. His résumé had just the right amount of experience; he'd grown up in the denomination; and best of all, he was joyful, charming, and wise during his phone interviews. Holy Oak Church was eager to fly him in for a visit. But St. Luke's, a church over 500 miles away, got to him first.

When Missy, the Holy Oak search committee chair, called Jimmy to arrange his visit, he said, "I don't want to waste your money and have you fly me out. I have decided to accept the call to St. Luke's."

When Missy told me about her conversation with Jimmy, I was curious. So I called him to find out a little about Jimmy's experience with St. Luke's. His story went something like this:

"I got in around midnight. The airline had lost my luggage," he said. "But a dad of one of the teenagers in the youth group picked me up. On the way to the hotel, he told me a little about the town, his family, and the church."

Jimmy went on to explain that the morning after his arrival, his luggage had been delivered, and Jimmy met with the Search Team for his formal interview at the church. After the interview, he had lunch with the senior pastor, who was enthusiastic about answering his questions.

There were several hours of free time in the afternoon, followed by a church dinner—a send-off for their associate pastor, who was leaving. "I got to meet a ton of people there," Jimmy said. And after the dinner, he went for an informal dessert at the home of a different youth family. "Before I could put the first bite of pie in my mouth," he said, "the mom said, 'We're not on the hiring committee, so if you have any questions, we can be very frank and honest with you.'" And they were. They didn't gloss over the fact that the youth ministry had struggled in the previous few years, and they knew it would take time to get things back on track again.

The next morning, a different family brought Jimmy to church. "After church," he said, "I talked with kids and parents in the youth room, basically another interview with them. I loved the fact that 20 random kids and 10 adults were involved in the interview process. It let me know that the church takes them seriously." After church, another family took Jimmy out to dinner and back to the airport.

Though not every successful on-site interview needs to mirror this experience, it is clear that St. Luke's leaders knew what they were doing and had a plan long before Jimmy arrived in their city. The biggest lesson our friends at Holy Oak learned from St. Luke's is that an on-site visit is not simply an interview; it is also a recruiting visit.

When candidates come for an on-site visit, you will want to give them an opportunity to fall in love with your church, your congregation, and your teenagers. The three most common things we hear from youth workers about how they choose their new church are these:

- "The church was a good fit. I felt like I belonged there."
- "I liked the town. I could see myself living there."
- "The church takes youth ministry seriously. I could see myself staying there."

Because this might very well be the last time you get the chance for face-to-face conversations before offering him or her the position, don't rush things or try to cram in back-to-back-to-back interviews. If you're serious about your final two or three candidates, you'll want to take at least day for each on-site interview—a good full day if they are local and at least 30 hours if they are coming from out of town.

Productive on-site interviews always start with a plan:

STEP 24: CREATE A SCHEDULE

Saturdays and Sundays can be great days for on-site interviews, giving candidates a good feel for the church's worship style and for what the church is like during its most intense programming time. Each church, of course, will design its own unique schedule for an on-site interview, but we have included a sample schedules in Appendix P to provide your Search Team with a starting point.

As you are building the schedule, you'll want to include

- the formal interview with the Search Team.
- time with the senior pastor or the person who will be the youth pastor's direct supervisor.
- formal and/or informal time with a few students, parents, and leaders whom you'd like to have involved in the process.
- the chance for the candidate to teach a group of students, especially if programming and/or teaching will be a heavy component of the youth pastor's job description.
- a tour of the church facility.
- some downtime for the candidate.

The on-site visit should include the chance for the Search Team to observe from a distance. Turn the candidate loose with a group of teenagers and parents and watch what happens. Does he or she mingle or simply gravitate toward one group and stay there? Does the candidate avoid either parents or students? Are people engaged by his or her conversation?

One of the most important keys to the schedule is ensuring that the only person who is "on" for the day or day and a half and is expected to be at everything on the schedule is the candidate. Other responsibilities can be divided among members of the Search Team and other volunteers, leaving no one volunteer overwhelmed.

STEP 25: ASSIGN A HOST

Once the schedule is set, you'll want to assign one person to serve as the candidate's host during the on-site interview. The host will take responsibility for ensuring that everything is in place to make each component of the schedule run smoothly. If there is a meal, the host ensures that arrangements have been made. If there are a group of parents and youth who will meet to interview the candidate, the host invites them. When meetings are to begin, the host ensures a comfortable, natural handoff of the candidate from one meeting to the next.

At least a week before the interview, the host will have sent the candidate a welcome package, including useful information about the church, the youth program, its vision, goals, calendars, and newsletters. Before the candidate arrives, the host will have been the candidate's primary contact person, ensuring that hotel reservations, flights, and airport pickups are all arranged. And once the candidate does arrive, the host is available by cell phone to solve any glitches that may come up in the schedule.

Though the host may be a member of the Search Team, the host role can be a wonderful opportunity to include a youth ministry stakeholder outside of the Search Team. You can have a single host who handles every on-site candidate, or you can have a different host for each candidate to make the workload more manageable.

Once the Search Team has developed a schedule for the visit and recruited a host, the team will send the host a copy of the schedule along with a copy of the host job description (for a sample, see Appendix O). If the Search Team is expecting the host to invite specific people to one or more events on the schedule, this information should be passed along to the host with the schedule and the job description.

STEP 26: RECRUIT THE NECESSARY PLAYERS

The key to a hernia-free on-site interview is ensuring that you have all the necessary players, each playing his or her small part well. Consider this checklist of possible volunteers you may want to get in place before the interview actually begins:

Transportation:

- ☐ Airport pickup
- ☐ Breakfast 1 pickup
- ☐ Lunch 1 pickup
- ☐ Dinner pickup
- ☐ Breakfast 2 pickup
- ☐ Lunch 2 pickup
- ☐ Airport drop-off

Meals:

- ☐ Arranger of meals in homes
- ☐ Arranger of meals at restaurant(s)
- ☐ Arranger of meals at church

Invitations:

- ☐ Inviter of students
- ☐ Inviter of parents
- ☐ Inviter of leaders

Follow-Up:

- ☐ The collector of impressions from students, leaders, parents, and staff
- ☐ The post-visit communicator with the candidate

A large team takes a little work from the Search Team's shoulders. More importantly, it exposes the candidate to a wide variety of people in the church, which can provide a more textured picture of the church and the opportunities for youth ministry.

STEP 27: ASK THE RIGHT QUESTIONS

Of course, the central component of the on-site visit is the actual interview with the Search Team. You'll want to make sure you have at least 90 minutes carved out for the interview, and follow these preparation tips to make that time as productive as possible:

1. Determine whether anyone else will be invited into the formal interview with the Search Team; as appropriate, appoint someone on the team to invite those people.
2. Establish the process for the meeting by answering the following questions:
    - Who will moderate the interview?
    - Which questions will be our preselected questions (the ones that must be asked in the interview)? You might, at this point, take another look at Appendix M to decide if you want to choose any questions that are different from the 10 you asked during the videoconferencing interview.
    - Which questions will we ask based on concerns raised from the résumé, the screening interview, and any background research and reference calls?
    - Who will ask which questions?
3. Determine how much time will be spent on each of the following components of the interview:
    - Introductions, including a general introduction to the youth ministry
    - Preselected questions the entire group agrees should be asked

- Questions raised from the résumé, reference checks, or screening calls
- Questions from the candidate to the Search Team
- General questions from the Search Team

Just as you did in the phone and video interviews, be honest. Show the church's warts and challenges, even while you're highlighting the church's strengths. If someone is going to be scared off by the tough things at your church, better for that happen before the person starts.

WOOING AND SCREENING

One Search Team member had an aha moment recently when she said to us, "I get it! It's like sorority rush!"

What she meant was that if you wait to encourage the candidate until you're absolutely sure you're going to offer the job, you've waited too long. So make sure you include downtime, with easygoing people. It gives your candidate a chance to relax and enjoy your community of faith. And at the same time, you get to see your candidate outside of "interview behavior." A lot can be learned from watching someone's behavior during a casual dinner or by walking through a park.

A great on-site interview doesn't simply send the candidate from interrogation to interrogation. You can get a lot of interviewing done in the car on the way to fun places. At the same time, when your candidate visits with lots of people during the on-site interview, in both formal and informal settings, there is a greater chance he or she will fall in love with your people, your vision, your town, and your church.

BEFORE YOU OFFER: SAVING TIME AND FRUSTRATION BY COMMUNICATING PROACTIVELY

CHAPTER 9

> "ONE OF OUR CHURCH'S BIGGEST WEAKNESSES IS COMMUNICATION. IN FACT, WE STINK AT IT."
>
> —SOMEONE IN ALMOST EVERY CHURCH WE'VE EVER VISITED

Anyone who has been part of a church's leadership for more than about 15 seconds can likely tell a tale of miscommunication, a time when a decision was made in one corner of the church but never got conveyed to the other corner. When we're in the thick of making important and urgent decisions, it's easy to forget someone who really needs to know.

"You canceled your fundraiser," Marcie said to the youth pastor, "and you never told the Finance Committee. We're the ones who approved it in the first place!"

"They quit meeting for the summer, but no one bothered to tell me," said Jim, the custodian.

"They offered this guy $30 per hour for part-time work! That's twice what any other part-timer at our church makes," said David, the executive pastor.

"I've had four weeks of vacation everywhere else I've ever worked," said Jim, the new youth pastor. "And now they're telling me I get five days after a year on the job? I wish I'd known that before I came. This is going to be a problem."

In each of these cases, the person who forgot to communicate could simply hang his head or smack his forehead and say, "Wow, I should have thought of that." But there is a better way.

As you move toward calling your next youth pastor, wouldn't it be great if all the key players were informed *before* the offer was made? That priority is the focus of this chapter.

STEP 28: CONFIRM YOUR NUMBERS

Before you can make a firm offer to your top candidate, you will need to confirm with the Finance Committee that the salary and benefit number that you are offering is within the approved range. You also want to confirm with the Personnel Committee that the vacation, continuing education, medical, and pension benefits are in-line with the benefit structure for other staff in the church (and if not, are approved as an exception).

STEP 29: GET YOUR PASSPORT STAMPED BY ALL THE PROPER AUTHORITIES

If there is any remaining confusion on this question, now is the time to make sure that the Search Team understands who in your church's system has the authority to make the offer to the top candidate. Is it the Search Team? Is it the Personnel Committee? Is it the lead pastor or the executive pastor?

If the answers to these questions are still unclear, ask your pastor. In most churches, pastors know exactly where the land mines are; they usually found out the hard way. It might also be prudent for the chair of your Search Team to have a confirming conversation with every person or committee that might feel snubbed by not being informed before an offer is made. These are not necessarily "permission-getting" calls; they are courtesy calls to formal or informal leaders who you want to make sure are as excited as you are about the coming of the new youth pastor.

The standard rule of communication is intensely true in the church: It's hard for people to be "up" on the things they are not up on. If you want the excitement about the new youth pastor to be virally contagious, it will be important to include the right people on the "inside track" before the offer is actually made. Without question, you'll want the following folks to sign off on the offer you plan to make, just to make sure the church has the capacity to deliver on the offer:

- ☐ Your pastor
- ☐ The new youth pastor's supervisor (if different from the pastor)
- ☐ The chair of the Personnel Committee
- ☐ The chair of the Finance Committee
- ☐ The representative of your church's governing board (if your church has one)

But it would also be wise to consider informing these people:

- ☐ Key volunteers
- ☐ A key parent or two
- ☐ A key teenager or two
- ☐ Anyone with "informal authority" in the church whose blessing will be important for the new youth pastor's enthusiastic reception
- ☐ The chair of the Youth Committee

Making all these calls can feel overwhelming if one person is responsible to make them all. But by dividing that responsibility among all the members of the team, with each person making a few calls, you'll be able to cover all the ground that needs to be covered in relatively short order.

STEP 30: MAKE A VERBAL OFFER

Once the Search Team is clear about the candidate you would like to call as your next youth pastor, you'll want to make a verbal offer to your top candidate. Ordinarily, this call would come from the chair of the Search Team, who would give specifics of the offer and answer any questions the candidate might have.

By the time you put the offer in writing, you would like to know that your new youth pastor has said yes or is going to say yes. It is a good idea to discover and work out any troublesome details before the written offer is sent, such as any difference in understanding about salary and benefits or about vacation or budget. There should be nothing surprising in the written offer.

STEP 31: PUT THE OFFER IN WRITING

Within 24 hours of reaching verbal agreement with the candidate that the terms of the offer are acceptable, go ahead and put the offer in writing. Don't trust the clarity of your mutual understanding to a firm handshake and good feelings. Get everyone on the same page by putting the offer in writing.

The written offer typically contains the following elements:

- **The Big Embrace:** The first paragraph should simply be a celebration of the upcoming partnership of God, your church, and your new youth pastor.
- **The Job Summary:** You will attach the job description, so there is no need to go into too much detail here. A sentence or two will suffice.
- **The Salary:** How much will it be, when do paydays occur, and how often will the youth pastor have the opportunity for a review and raise?
- **The Benefits:** Review the health plan, vacation, and any unique benefits like moving expenses and continuing education funds. If your church has an employees' manual, you can highlight a few points in the letter, then refer your new youth pastor to the manual for more details.
- **The Start Date:** You are eagerly awaiting the day your new youth pastor starts in his or her new position, and you specifically identify that date in the letter.

You can find a sample offer letter in Appendix Q.

ALMOST THERE

Many Search Teams assume that by the time they reach this point in the process, their job is done. Well, almost. There is one more crucial piece of the puzzle that can shave months off of the learning curve for your new youth pastor.

BEFORE YOUR YOUTH PASTOR ARRIVES: SETTING UP YOUR NEW STAFF FOR SUCCESS

CHAPTER 10

["FIRST IMPRESSIONS MATTER WHEN YOU WANT TO BUILD A LASTING TRUST. IF YOU GET OFF ON THE WRONG FOOT, THE RELATIONSHIP MAY NEVER BE COMPLETELY RIGHT AGAIN. IT'S EASIER TO REBUILD TRUST AFTER A BREACH IF YOU ALREADY HAVE A STRONG RELATIONSHIP."

—ROBERT LOUNT, PROFESSOR AND RESEARCHER AT OHIO STATE UNIVERSITY]

I asked Jim to tell me how his first week at Grace Church went.

"To tell you the truth, it was pretty frustrating," he said. "Let's just say we've got some *communication* issues here."

He spent about 15 minutes getting some things off his chest. "My office doesn't have a computer." ("They" were looking for a used one among the congregation members). "But that's OK," he continued, "because there's no place to put a computer anyway." He did have a newly painted office, but all the furniture had been moved out to make room for the new furniture that would be ordered as soon as the trustee, who was an expert in interior design, got back from vacation to approve the purchase.

"I'm not sure anyone knows who I am yet," Jim continued. "The pastor was supposed to introduce me in the worship service, but he said that the service was too packed last week. So I'm just introducing myself to everything that moves. A few people have figured out that we have a new youth pastor!"

"But that's OK," Jim laughed nervously. "If they had it all together, they wouldn't have needed me!"

Jim's church missed some incredible opportunities: the opportunity to build enthusiasm for its youth and their families and the opportunity to accelerate Jim's impact in the church. Unfortunately, Jim's story is all too common.

Exhausted Search Team members are thrilled with the youth director arrives. Other people are busy doing the things that have been keeping them busy for years, and no one takes the time to ensure that the new hire launches well. And the new youth director is left wondering whom he can count on when (not if) things really get hard.

After you offer a job to a candidate and he or she has arrived on the scene, there are still some things that must be done. As exciting as it is for you and as nervous as you might be about a new hire, the new youth pastor has all those feelings and more. So one of the Search Team's final tasks is to help ease the transition into this new community of faith.

Zig Ziglar, one of the great salesmen of the 20th century, once said that when it comes to marriage, "Most guys are great at closing the sale, but they do a terrible job of following up with the account."

Churches that do the follow-up work well increase a new youth pastor's impact, shorten his or her learning curve, and convince the new hire that he or she has made a great choice accepting this job. So before you disband the Search Team, you'll want to put just a few things in place.

STEP 32: ESTABLISH A PRE-ARRIVAL COMMUNICATION POINT PERSON

The time between when your new youth pastor says "yes" to the position and when he or she actually begins in the new job could be months—months when the new youth pastor will likely have many questions. Someone from the Search Team should serve as the link between the new youth pastor and all the resources he or she might need before starting on the job. This will not likely require lots of hours, but it can do wonders to help the new youth pastor stay connected and supported during the interim weeks or months.

STEP 33: ARRANGE FOR A RETURN VISIT

Since often the only time your new youth pastor was on-site before being hired was the interview, there is a good chance that there will be a few logistical details that will need to be worked out before his or her fist day of work. Ordinarily, these details are worked out on a return visit to your church.

It will be helpful for someone to serve as the return visit coordinator. Again, this could be someone on the Search Team or someone else from the church who is well-connected in the community.

The first responsibility for the return visit coordinator should be to call your new youth pastor and discover the desired outcomes for the visit by asking the following questions:

- Are you hoping to find a house to purchase on this visit, or are you looking for a place to rent until you get a better feel for the city?
- If you are hoping to buy, would you like us to locate a real estate agent who can spend some time with you on your visit?
- Is there anyone else you would like to meet with while you're in town? Doctors? School principals? Other youth workers in the community?
- Where would you like to stay when you are in town—in a hotel, at the home of someone at a similar stage in life, or the home of someone you met on the last visit?
- Is there anything else you would like to accomplish while you are in town?
- How long would you like the visit to last?
- Would you like us to take care of flight arrangements (if applicable), or would you like to book your own flight?
- Will anyone else from your family be coming with you?

If you are hiring an ordained youth pastor, there may be a need to coordinate his or her visit with a meeting of a denominational body or denominational executive. The return visit coordinator will want to check with the pastor to see if there are any such meetings that need to be built into the schedule. The pastor may also have suggestions of other priorities to be accomplished on this visit.

Once the return visit coordinator has a sense of the needs for the return visit, he or she can draft a schedule, making sure to include downtime in the schedule. Once that schedule is approved by the new youth pastor, the return visit coordinator can work to ensure that all the pieces are in place for a welcoming and productive return visit.

STEP 34: CREATE A NEW ARRIVAL CHECKLIST

We have created a new arrival checklist (see Appendix R) to help your team get started on the bases you'll want to cover before your new youth pastor launches. Your team will want certainly want to make additions and edits to the checklist we have provided; we simply want to prompt your team to think about tasks that you might never consider otherwise.

STEP 35: RECRUIT A WELCOME COORDINATOR

Before your new youth pastor arrives in town, you'll want to recruit someone to serve as the welcome coordinator for him or her. Again, this may be someone on the Search Team or could be someone highly invested in the youth ministry who has the gifts to coordinate all the details to welcoming the new youth pastor.

Among other things, the welcome coordinator oversees the new arrival checklist (see Appendix R). This usually begins at one of the last meetings of the Search Team, when each item on the checklist is assigned to someone on the Search Team with a specific deadline.

Not all of the items on the checklist will need to be accomplished by someone on the Search Team, but someone on the Search Team will have responsibility to ensure that his or her assigned items actually get accomplished. For example, it will not likely be someone on the Search Team who actually places the new youth pastor's picture on the website, but the Search Team member can work with the appropriate people at church to make sure it happens. It will be the key job of the welcome coordinator to make sure that all the responsibilities assigned to various members of the Search Team are taken care of on or before their assigned deadlines.

STEP 36: PROTECT YOUR INVESTMENT

After observing countless job searches and their long-term outcomes, we know that most of these new relationships blossom into something wonderfully fruitful and fulfilling. In a few cases, though, we've seen optimism fade and wither. Sometimes, there was just a misunderstanding or a bad fit. In some cases, someone forgot to ask an important question, or a candidate said, "Yes, I believe X," when he or she should have said, "No, I believe Y."

No search process, no matter how thorough, can ensure a perfect fit. What we have found, though, is that a church can create the right kind of soil in which a new youth pastor can thrive by taking responsibility for three key areas.

BE A CHURCH WITH CLEAR EXPECTATIONS

A church that says "No one around here really cares about numbers" is kidding itself. Our experience, after working with more than 200 churches, is that every church has a minimum threshold of youth ministry attendance, youth ministry programs, and a level of enthusiasm that must be met or exceeded. Youth ministers who "pay these rents" tend to have much greater freedom to be creative, take risks, and experiment with innovative ideas. And those that fail to pay these rents often find themselves mired in distrust, second-guessing, and discouragement. The key is to name the expectations in clear, measureable terms so everyone who cares can know what the official expectations are. Without clear expectations, the youth pastor will be judged on 50 different scales by 50 different people.

"We want to see more outreach" means one thing at St. John's Episcopal Church in Boston and something quite different at Hillside Baptist in the mountains of North Carolina. You'll want to take the time to clarify the meaning of any commonly used Christian terminology with your new youth pastor.

BE A CHURCH WITH RESOURCES TO MATCH YOUR EXPECTATIONS

One day, Jesus told a story about a builder, a story that has something important to tell us about building a thriving youth ministry:

"But don't begin until you count the cost. For who would begin construction of a building without first calculating the cost to see if there is enough money to finish it? Otherwise, you might complete only the foundation before running out of money, and then everyone would laugh at you. They would say, 'There's the person who started that building and couldn't afford to finish it!'" (Luke 14:28-30).

After working for almost a decade consulting churches in their youth ministries, our YMA team has developed a pretty good feel for "the cost" of a healthy youth ministry. These are the basic rules of thumb:

- **Staff:** Plan on one full-time staff person for every 50 youth that you want to see involved in some aspect of your youth ministry each week. The staff doesn't replace volunteers; it coordinates, trains, and supports them.

- **Volunteers:** We like to think in terms of "spans of care," recognizing that most volunteers cannot effectively oversee the church's Christian nurture of more than about five students on an ongoing basis. So if you have a ratio of less than one volunteer for every five students, there is still some investment to be made.

- **Budget:** Since this one is driven largely by your budget for staff, it can vary based on the cost of living in your community. We have found, however, that $1,000-$1,500 X the number of students active on an average week is a good rule of thumb to start from (at least at the time of this writing). In other words, if your church wants to build a youth ministry that reaches 50 teenagers every week, you can expect to spend about $50,000 per year in salaries, benefits, and program expenses.

  Churches that fail to match their expectations and their investment often find themselves churning in a climate of criticism and burnout for staff and volunteers. Underinvested youth ministries are usually characterized by programs that start, sputter, and then stop. As a result, the least expensive approach to youth ministry can often be the most costly.

BE A CHURCH THAT PROVIDES SUPERVISION, COACHING, AND TRAINING APPROPRIATE TO THE YOUTH PASTOR'S LEVEL OF EXPERIENCE

If you've hired a rookie, you'll want to make sure plans are in place for his or her ongoing coaching and training. The typical training plan for inexperienced youth pastors has been to throw them into the pool and hope they can swim (maybe with the help of an annual youth ministry convention). But your church can do better.

If your church has decided to hire a young, enthusiastic, but relatively inexperienced youth pastor, you have also committed to being an incubator for his or her growing ministry. You will want to make sure that your new youth pastor has a youth ministry mentor, whether on staff, an effective youth worker in town, or a youth ministry consultant. This investment may be one of the best you make in your youth ministry. In the *Before You Hire a Youth Pastor Resource Pack*, we have provided a checklist of items normally covered in a half-day quick start with a new staff person.

Over the years, we've been delighted to watch the lengthening tenure of the youth workers we coach. There is undeniably something about having a youth ministry veteran coach readily available that provides a pressure valve in situations that might easily be overwhelming.

If you've hired someone with proven experience, you'll want to let him or her swim! The seasoned veteran should know that higher expectations are part of the package. Once the new youth pastor understands the church's culture and vision, and once clear accountability systems are in place, you'll want to give room so that to make his or her own mark and make honest mistakes.

While you'll want to take the initiative to provide mentoring and coaching for a rookie youth worker, you'll want to ask your veteran youth worker what sort of professional support would feel most helpful to him or her.

We work with one experienced youth pastor who explains our relationship this way: "Even Tiger Woods has a swing coach." If your new, experienced youth pastor requests a "swing coach," by all means, you'll want to find a way to provide such a thing!

STEP 37: SCHEDULE FIRST-YEAR QUARTERLY CHECK-INS WITH YOUR NEW YOUTH PASTOR

Instead of assuming that everything will go perfectly in the coming year, it will be helpful for your team to schedule quarterly check-in meetings with your new youth pastor during the first year. These meetings can be as informal as a dinner at one of your houses or can formally involve members of your church's youth committee or pastoral staff.

Though your team will have no authority to make changes, you can provide a listening ear and help your youth pastor navigate some of the unique challenges of the first year of ministry more effectively.

STEP 38: CELEBRATE. YOU DID IT!

NOW THAT YOU'RE FINISHED

EPILOGUE

["ONE DAY SOMEONE ELSE WILL BE DOING WHAT YOU ARE DOING. WHETHER YOU HAVE AN EXIT STRATEGY OR NOT, ULTIMATELY, YOU WILL EXIT."

—ANDY STANLEY, REGGIE JOINER, AND LANE JONES, ***SEVEN PRACTICES OF EFFECTIVE MINISTRY***]

By the time you have reached the end of your search, if you're like most teams that have worked this process, you built a surprising number of friendships with others on your team—those who have walked this journey with you for the past few months. You may be just a little bit amazed that the process actually worked! And you're likely ready for a little well-deserved rest.

Thank you for the countless hours you invested, not only in finding a youth pastor who is a great fit for your ministry but also in helping your church lay the foundation for a sustainable youth ministry, one that can last even beyond the tenure of the newest member of your youth staff. Over the next few years, your church and likely some of your children will enjoy the fruit of your faithful labor. Thank you.

We would love to hear your search story, so if you have one to share, you can do so at info@ymarchitects.com. And if our Youth Ministry Architects team can ever be of assistance helping your church move through its current or future transitions in youth ministry, we would love to hear from you (YMArchitects.com or info@ymarchitects.com).

The next chapter is for your church and your new youth pastor to write together.

ENDNOTES

1. Lyle E. Schaller, *Mainline Turnaround: Strategies for Congregations and Denominations* (Nashville, TN: Abingdon Press, 2005).

2. Mike Woodruff, *Managing Youth Ministry Chaos* (Loveland, CO: Group Publishing, 2000).

3. Jim Collins, *Good to Great and the Social Sectors: A Monograph to Accompany Good to Great* (New York, NY: HarperCollins, 2005).

4. Rosabeth Moss Kanter, *Confidence: How Winning Streaks and Losing Streaks Begin and End* (New York, NY: Crown Business, 2004).

5. Merton P. Strommen, Karen Jones, and Dave Rahn, *Youth Ministry That Transforms* (Grand Rapids, MI: Zondervan, 2001).

6. Brian Tracy, *Eat That Frog!: 21 Great Ways to Stop Procrastinating and Get More Done in Less Time* (San Francisco, CA: Berrett-Koehler Publishers, 2002).

7. Thom Rainer and Eric Geiger, *Simple Church: Returning to God's Process for Making Disciples* (Nashville, TN: B&H Books, 2006).

A QUICK WORD ON THE APPENDICES

The following Appendices are available for your use as your church goes through the necessary steps to hiring the right youth pastor. These files, and a whole lot more, are also available on a supplemental resource called the *Before You Hire a Youth Pastor Resource Pack*. This resource pack contains all of these forms and more in an editable Microsoft Word® document to help you customize the material to fit your church and ministry needs. The resource pack is available as a CD-ROM or as a download at simplyyouthministry.com.

JOB DESCRIPTION FOR THE SEARCH TEAM

APPENDIX A

Thank you for agreeing to take the lead on this job search. I'm sure you were already a busy person before you ever said yes, so our church appreciates your willingness to serve teenagers and their families. You can expect this process to take at least six months. Thank you for making this significant commitment to the future of our youth ministry.

Mission: Assist and counsel the ___________ (insert Pastor, Associate Pastor, Session, Personnel Committee) in finding the person God is calling to be the next ____________ (insert appropriate title) for our church.

Essential Responsibilities:

- **Problem solving:** In consultation with the _____________ (insert Pastor, Associate Pastor, Session, Personnel Committee), develop timely, creative solutions to challenges that might arise related to the search for a youth director.
- **Establishing and managing the search timeline:** Using the timeline found in the *Before You Hire a Youth Pastor Resource Pack* as a starting point, the Search Team will create its own timeline and assign responsibilities for achieving the various responsibilities outlined in the timeline. This process will involve the Search Team meeting regularly for the duration of the search.
- **Clarifying the job description:** The Search Team will first ensure that the job description is clear and lines up with the church's established vision and goals for its youth ministry.

- **Carrying the load:** The Search Team will accomplish the upfront legwork, including beating the bushes and collecting and filtering résumés.

- **Beating the bushes:** More than 150 contacts (people who might know of good candidates for the position) will be made by the members of the Search Team or by congregation members recruited by the Search Team. The goal of each call is to come away with two kinds of names and contact information: possible candidates for the position or other contacts who might know of good candidates.

- **Collecting and filtering résumés:** Every résumé received will be read and graded by the Search Team, resulting in a list of Top 5 to 7 résumés for review by the __________ (insert Pastor, Associate Pastor, Session, Personnel Committee).

- **Interviewing:** Search Team members will participate in the phone interviews, in-person interviews, and reference checks for the top candidates. They will counsel the final decision makers in selecting the top candidate.

- **Prayer:** Knowing that this is more than a job search—it is a process of discernment and God's calling—Search Team members will regularly keep this process in their prayers.

SURVEY FOR EXAMINING YOUR STAFF STRUCTURE

APPENDIX B

Answering this simple, three-question survey can save your church hundreds of hours and thousands of dollars by helping your team build a solid structure for sustainability for your next youth pastor.

1. Who will take responsibility for creating, revising, and editing the *design* for the youth ministry?

    - Someone currently on our staff who will be supervising the youth ministry; this person has proven experience in creating and implementing strategic plans.
    - The person we are hiring (likely an expensive one) will have proven experience in creating and implementing strategic plans.
    - A volunteer in our church who has time and proven experience in creating and implementing strategic plans and who can take responsibility for leading youth ministry stakeholders in the church through this process.
    - An outside consultant with proven experience in creating and implementing strategic plans for youth ministries.

2. Who will take responsibility for coordinating the details related to the youth ministry, particularly the recruitment and coordination of volunteers?

    - We would like our ministry to remain small enough (fewer than 50 teenagers) that our new youth director can carry the responsibility for coordinating all the details related to the youth ministry.

- We will hire (or have hired) someone for the youth ministry staff who is charged with responsibility to initiate coordinating the flow of work related to the youth ministry, not a secretarial or administrative assistant role.
- We have an incredible volunteer who can give more than 20 hours a week and who is willing to take responsibility for managing all the details related to the youth ministry.

3. Which of the following youth ministry responsibilities will be considered a core responsibility of the new youth staff person: Relational Ministry, Creative Programming, Event Management, Volunteer Training, Ministry to Parents of Youth?

   - With additional staff in place to handle the strategic design of the youth ministry and the management of the logistics of the ministry, the new youth staff person will be expected to handle all of these five responsibilities.
   - Since it is our expectations that the total scope of our youth ministry will not reach beyond 50 active students weekly, we will expect our next youth staff person to handle all strategic and logistical aspects of the youth ministry, as well as the above five areas. But we recognize that it is highly unlikely that we will hire someone who will be excellent in all these areas and plan to identify our new youth worker's areas of strength and build systems to help cover the two or three areas where he or she may be less proficient.
   - We have selected three of the above five areas on which we expect our new youth staff person to focus.

Did your answers to these three questions lead you to the same staffing structure that you have had in the recent past or to the staffing structure for which you are now hiring? One of the Search Team's roles is to make sure that the staff position you are about to hire matches the church's expectations and investment. If that is not the case, pause now and rethink the position.

RESULTS-BASED JOB DESCRIPTION: FULL-TIME YOUTH PASTOR (NON-ORDAINED)

APPENDIX C

Position Summary: The Youth Pastor reports directly to the Senior Pastor and will be directly responsible for:

1. Overseeing the youth ministry of *(insert name of church)* and directing the implementation of its mission and vision.
2. Assisting in the implementation of a restructuring plan for the youth ministry in conjunction with the Renovation Team and adult volunteers.
3. Spiritually preparing the youth of *(insert name of church)* for challenges ahead in young adulthood and nurturing in those youth a sense of clear Christian identity through an understanding of God-given gifts and talents.

RESPONSIBILITIES:

RELATIONSHIPS: The first priority of the Youth Pastor is to ensure that relationships are being built between the adult leaders of *(insert name of church)* and the youth of the church.

- **Result #1:** The Youth Pastor knows 90 percent of the youth in the youth directory by name as well as their parents.
- **Result #2:** All first-time guests to youth events are receiving exceptional and timely follow-up, so that all youth who want to become a part of the *(insert name of church)* youth ministry do so in a way that feels welcoming and natural to them.

- **Result #3:** The Youth Pastor serves as a “sounding board” for students and their parents and has an accessible referral list of professional counselors to access when necessary.
- **Result #4:** The Youth Pastor is participating weekly in community and/or school events involving youth connected with the *(insert name of church)* youth ministry.
- **Result #5:** “Spontaneous” events are engaging not only the participating youth, but also youth from the community and from *(insert name of church)* families who have not been regularly participating.

RECRUITING and SUPERVISION: The Youth Pastor coordinates and supervises all youth ministry staff and hands-on adult volunteers regularly to ensure that the efforts of all adult leaders and staff members are coordinated to maximize their effectiveness.

- **Result #6:** All weekly hands-on adult volunteers are recruited and have received training at least one month before their terms of service began.
- **Result #7:** Regular meetings, in which support, training, and encouragement are provided to the volunteers working hands-on with youth, are taking place.
- **Result #8:** The Youth Pastor has protected the strategic progress of the *(insert name of church)* youth ministry by ensuring that (1) three-year goals and one-year benchmarks for the youth ministry are updated annually, (2) the youth staff annually evaluates progress based on those goals and benchmarks, and (3) the staff is regularly attentive to accomplishing the youth ministry’s one-year benchmarks.

PROGRAMS: The Youth Pastor ensures that all details of youth programs and special events are taken care of so that an atmosphere of belonging and fellowship is created, in which emerging spiritual and leadership skills can be developed.

- **Result #9:** The weekly programs (such as Sunday morning classes, youth group, and small groups) are growing in participation, enthusiasm, and excellence.
- **Result #10:** A curriculum design template is in place for the *(insert name of church)* youth ministry, and curriculum resources for each year are selected at least one month before the school year begins.
- **Result #11:** All major events coordinators and other behind-the-scenes volunteers are being recruited and equipped with the information and tools needed to carry out their responsibilities.
- **Result #12:** The youth ministry regularly has met or exceeded its participation targets for calendared youth ministry events.
- **Result #13:** The Youth Pastor is available to teach Sunday morning classes when needed and is present on Sunday mornings in worship and around the Sunday school classrooms.
- **Result #14:** The Youth Pastor is ensuring that adherence to the Safe Sanctuary policy of *(insert name of church)* is being followed in all youth programs.
- **Result #15:** Expenses for the current year are being tracked, and a budget for the coming year is proposed to the leadership of the church as requested.

SUPERVISORY RESPONSIBILITIES

QUALIFICATIONS

EDUCATION:

- Undergraduate degree, and Master of Divinity Degree

EXPERIENCE:

- At least five years' experience leading a youth ministry involving at least 100 youth.

KNOWLEDGE:

- Knowledge of Bible, theology, Presbyterian polity, pastoral theology, spiritual formation.

ABILITIES:

- Initiative, leadership, ability to connect well with youth and volunteers, problem solving, patience, teaching, preaching, writing, reading, sense of humor, empathy, energy. Ability to communicate effectively in oral and written form. Ability to prioritize and balance multiple tasks and manage potentially tense political situations. Commitment to grow as a disciple of Christ.

CERTIFICATES, LICENSES, REGISTRATIONS

- M.Div. Degree from an accredited school
- Satisfactory completion of ordination examinations

PHYSICAL DEMANDS

The typical youth staff member will endure a number of nights each year with minimal sleep, particularly on retreats and trips with students. In addition, there will be seasons when the physical demands of the youth ministry can be exhausting, particularly when preparing for a major event or multiple major events. Assisting event volunteers with cleanup and staff clean-up days (which take place multiple times through the year) can require some heavy lifting as the staff person's ability allows.

WORK ENVIRONMENT

In addition to programs that take place on the grounds of the church and in the homes of members, much of the work of the Youth Pastor will require work that takes place away from the office.

RESULTS-BASED JOB DESCRIPTION: PART-TIME YOUTH PROGRAM COORDINATOR

APPENDIX D

The Youth Program Coordinator helps the youth ministry accomplish *(insert youth ministry mission statement)* by serving in a part-time capacity to handle the day-to-day operation of the youth ministry. This position is mainly administrative and deals with the behind-the-scenes tasks that support the youth ministry.

DESCRIPTION AND RESPONSIBILITIES:

- **Result #1:** All major events are well-publicized and organized. Their execution leaves parents confident that their youth are being faithfully and creatively nurtured.
- **Result #2:** Event coordinators and volunteers have received appropriate support in order to serve the youth ministry. Their experience leaves them feeling that they've made a difference, and they are eager to serve with the youth ministry in the future.
- **Result #3:** Control documents are in place and distributed in a timely fashion (including the Youth Directory, Volunteer Job Descriptions, the Youth Ministry Calendar, Calendar Requests, Event and Trip Registration Forms, and Leaders Directory). Compliance documents are up to date and distributed to all involved parties (copyright licensing, background checks on volunteers and staff, and so on).
- **Result #4:** The "in-between-the-cracks" needs of the youth ministry are handled in a professional and timely manner (being distributed to other staff or volunteers). These needs include at least:

- Bulletin Boards, Photography, and Attendance Tracking
- Newsletters, Bulletin, and Sunday School Announcements
- Forms and Registrations
- Database and Website

- **Result #5:** The Youth Program Coordinator has ensured that event notebooks are completed for each major event and that each notebook is updated after the event is completed.
- **Result #6:** At least 75 percent of student parents on the rolls of the church are known by name by the Youth Program Coordinator.
- **Result #7:** All first-time guests receive exceptional and timely follow-up, so that all students who want to become a part of the *(insert church name)* youth ministry do so in a way that feels welcoming and natural to them.
- **Result #8:** Electronic copies of all job descriptions are updated, filed appropriately, and easily distributed to volunteers.
- **Result #9:** Attendance at regular meetings such as weekly staff meetings, appropriate committee meetings, and semi/monthly supervisory meetings with *(insert supervisor's title)* is occurring. Communication and coordination of these meetings as well as keeping minutes are taking place in a timely fashion. Informational and organizational support to appropriate committees is provided.

Team Composition (number): 1

Weekly Time Commitment: 20 hours

Special Talents, Skills Preferred: A goal-oriented individual who possesses the following traits: maturity, organization, self-starter capabilities, a warm personality, strong communication skills, motivation, administration skills, and the ability to meet deadlines.

Spiritual Gifts: Any of the following: *(Note: Erase the ones that don't apply)* Administration, Artistic Expression, Discernment, Helps, Intercession, Leadership, Mercy, Prophecy, Teaching, Hospitality

Resources and Training Provided: Attend semi-annual volunteer training events and the annual Safe Sanctuary training.

SOURCER'S JOB DESCRIPTION

APPENDIX E

Objective: To contact as many people as possible to find out if they know someone who might be interested in the position at your church; to find out who else you should be talking to about publicizing the position.

Reporting: All results should go back to the Sourcing Coordinator, who will report significant information to the Search Committee.

Responsibilities

- Summarize the strengths and the challenges of the church in a few sentences
- Articulate the qualifications for the position in a few sentences
- Contact list of sources, in addition to any assigned names
- Follow up (by phone or e-mail) with any names received from sources
- Convey all significant information to the Sourcing Coordinator

WHERE TO POST YOUR JOB OPENING

APPENDIX F

There are dozens if not hundreds of places for you to post your job opening. Websites for posting youth ministry jobs often change, and new ones spring up every year. Your team will want to use a search engine to discover the best places to post your opening. Here are a few of our favorites.

FREE INTERDENOMINATIONAL SITES

Simply Youth Ministry	simplyyouthministrytools.com/jobs
Youth Specialties	youthspecialties.com/jobs
Youth Ministry Architects	ymarchitects.com
Before You Hire a Youth Pastor	HireAYouthPastor.com

FREE DENOMINATIONAL SITES

Most denominations offer a job posting service at the national level. Ease of use and effectiveness vary. Here are a few of the more active sites:

American Anglican Council	americananglican.org/clergy-position-openings
Episcopalian	www.episcopalchurch.org (search for "youth formation job")
Evangelical Presbyterian	www.EPC.org (click on Opportunity List)
Lutheran ELCA	www.elcaymnet.org/Placement

Presbyterian (PCUSA)	www.pywa.org/job_board
Southern Baptist	www.sbc.net/jobs/
United Methodist	www.umc.org (type "youth job" in the site's search box)

ADDITIONAL POSTING SOURCES

- Contact the career development offices at nearby colleges, universities, and seminaries.
- Contact the publications (web and print) of the regional offices of your denomination.

FEE-BASED SITES

Our experience is that paid sites do not offer any better or worse results than the free sites. If you want to make sure you have all the bases covered, consider investing in one of these.

- ChristianJobs.com
- ChurchStaffing.com
- craigslist.com

CANDIDATE TRACKING SPREADSHEET

APPENDIX G

Information about every résumé received and every potential candidate should be included in the Candidate Tracking Spreadsheet. This document will not only allow you to keep track of the candidates, but it will also help the Search Team keep track of its tasks.

This list is maintained by the Candidate Tracker, updated and distributed weekly to all Search Team members. Your church might want to add or delete columns to match your search process.

It works especially well in Microsoft Word or Excel. You will want to use the "sort" function of your software from time to time, for example, to separate the résumés that are no longer being considered.

Name of Church

Type...

1 = One of the top candidates
2 = Maybe
3 = No thanks
99 = No longer available

Type	Name	1st contact from him/her	1st contact from us	Team has résumé	Denomination	Town	College grad year	Notes/ Experience	Comments from Search Team	Outcome	E-mail	Phone

CORRESPONDENCE: LETTER TO INDIVIDUALS WHO SEND RÉSUMÉS

APPENDIX H

When a person sends a résumé, the Search Team should immediately send a reply e-mail (or letter on church letterhead), letting the individual know that you received the résumé and explaining when to expect to hear more from your committee.

Here is a draft of what you might send. Feel free to change it to sound more like you and your situation:

Dear ______________________________,

Thank you for sending your résumé to us at __________________ *(your church)*. We will continue to receive résumés until ______________ *(date)*, at which time we will do the hard work of choosing our top five candidates. We will be sure to let you know the results of the decision. If you do not hear from us by that time, please feel free to check in and see where we are in the process.

Thank you for your commitment to Christ and youth. Blessings on your own discernment process.

Sincerely,

Your Name

Search Team member

If a person does not send a résumé but asks for information, try to answer any specific questions the individual has, within reason. You may want to send a copy of the job description. You definitely want to request a résumé.

Send an e-mail (or letter on church letterhead) saying something like this:

Dear ___________________________,

Thanks for your interest in the youth director position at _______________ *(your church)*. We are excited about what is going on with our youth ministry, and we can't wait to find the person God has in mind to lead our youth.

(Respond to any easy-to-answer questions). (Add if necessary:) I'm not sure I can answer all your questions, but I can ask about them.

I have attached a copy of our job description, which I think you will find helpful. If it looks like a good match for you, please send us your résumé.

Our Search Team is collecting résumés and hopes to select the top five to seven candidates by _______________________. If you do not hear from us by that time, please feel free to check in and see where we are in the process.

Thanks for serving God and loving teenagers.

Sincerely,

Your Name

Search Team member

OVERVIEW AND OUTLINE FOR THE INITIAL SCREENING CALL FOR TOP 5 CANDIDATES

APPENDIX I

Overview: The primary purpose of a screening phone interview is to identify any red flags that might cause the Search Team to choose not to schedule a video interview with this particular candidate. Even for those candidates who will continue on the Top 5 list and onto the video interview, the screening call can provide helpful information for the Search Team as it prepares for that interview. The screening should normally last around 15 minutes and serves as preparation for a more thorough one-hour video interview. (For more information on the screening process, see Chapter 7 of *Before You Hire a Youth Pastor*.)

At the end of the screening interview, you'll want to pass along the following information to the Phone Interview Coordinator or the chair of the Search Team:

Include at the top of your notes one of these two summaries:

- I recommend we continue pursuing ____________________ as a candidate because…
- I recommend we do not continue pursuing ________________ as a candidate because…

List any nagging concerns you sensed at the end of the interview.

List any additional means of learning more about the candidate: Facebook®, Twitter®, and so on.

Outline for the Screening Call:

1. Congratulate the candidate on being one of the top candidates selected by your Search Team.
2. Explain that you have just a few questions for this phone call:
    - *What about youth ministry do you love doing?*
    - *What parts of youth ministry are you not so crazy about?*
3. Ask any questions that arise based on the candidate's résumé. For example:
    - *Can you tell me a little bit about the short period of time you served at the last church?*
    - *As I look at your employment history, there seems to be a one-year gap. Can you tell me a little about that?*
    - *What has led to you feeling called to youth ministry after two decades in retail work?*
    - *I notice there are no references from your last church. Is there someone there we could talk to about your experience there?*
4. Give the candidate your Search Team's elevator speech about your position, your church, and the desired candidate, and ask:
    - *What about this position feels like a match for your gifts?*
    - *What about this position gives you cause for concern?*
5. Invite the candidate to ask any questions he or she might have. (Be prepared to say, "I don't know, but I can find out.")
6. Ask about additional resources for getting to know the candidate:
    - *Do you have a blog? If so, could you e-mail me a link?*
    - *Could we "friend you" on Facebook®?*
    - *Do you use Twitter®? If so, could we follow you?*

7. Ask for names and contact information for references if they were not included in the résumé. Be prepared to offer an e-mail address or phone number for the candidate to send that information to you at a later time.

8. Explain the next step in your process and when it will happen. Possible options:

   - *We would like to schedule a video interview with you. Is there a time that would be good for you?*

   - *We hope to select our top candidates by the end of the month, so you should hear something from us by then.*

9. Thank the candidate for the time spent with you.

REJECTION LETTER

APPENDIX J

Dear *(name of candidate)*,

On behalf of the Search Team of *(name of church)*, I want to thank you for your interest in the *(youth ministry position title)* position. Although the committee was very impressed with your background and experience, we have decided to pursue other applicants who more closely reflect the needs for the position.

I wish you continued blessings on your journey as you pursue God's call in life.

Sincerely,

Name

Search Team

Name of Church

REFERENCE PHONE CALLING GUIDE

APPENDIX K

Thanks for being willing to call references for one or more of the top candidates in our youth ministry search. Here are a few tips to make your calls more productive:

1. Take a minute to read through Chapter 7, particularly Steps 20 and 21, in *Before You Hire a Youth Pastor*.
2. Be prepared to leave several messages before you actually talk to the person making the reference.
3. As much as possible, keep your conversation to around 15 minutes.
4. Let the reference person know that you are both on the same side. They like the candidate; so do you—he or she made the Top 5 list. The message is that the candidate is a person of great value. We just don't want to saddle the candidate with a job that will create misery or set him or her up for failure.
5. Use the script supplied by the Search Team as an outline for your phone call.
6. In order to keep our search process moving according to schedule, we're asking that you shoot for completing your reference call within one week of being assigned the call.
7. You'll want to ask the chair of the Search Team for a copy of the "elevator speech" that defines the position and the kind of person the church is looking for.

8. Turn in a one-page summary of information gained from your reference call to the Search Team chair.

9. Make sure you end the call by thanking the reference and affirming something positive about the candidate.

SKELETON SCRIPT FOR REFERENCE PHONE CALLS

APPENDIX L

Hello, my name is ______________ and I'm with ___________________ church.

We're talking with _____________________ about a position with our youth ministry. He/she is one of our favorite candidates, and he/she gave your name as a reference. Do you have a few minutes to talk now, or can I make an appointment to call you back?

(If the reference person is available, ask the following questions):

- Can you tell me a little bit about how you know _________?
- I'm assuming you know a little something about his or her work in youth ministry. Could you give me your observations?
- How would you describe _______________'s personality?
- What can you tell me about _____________'s faith and how he or she expresses it?

(If the reference person has no personal knowledge of the candidate's ministry experience, you can skip the next question).

- To your knowledge, what responsibilities did his or her previous youth ministry job entail?
- Can you give me your impressions of what kind of a job he/she did?
- If I could talk to parents of the students ______________________ has worked with, what would they likely tell me?

- In _______________'s previous youth ministry position, what would you say would be his/her most significant achievement?

(You may want to follow up here by asking, "Can you tell me a little more about...")

- The purpose in our search isn't just to fill a slot but to find a good match for the position that our church has.
    - Having said that, would you think _______________ would flourish better in a job that emphasized organizational tasks or relationship tasks?
    - Would you expect him/her to be better in small group settings or in big group settings?
    - What parts of a normal youth ministry position (as you imagine it) might _______________ struggle with?
- Would you have any reservations about ________ working with your own child?
- Let me tell you a little about the position and the person we are looking for:

(Give the Search Team's elevator speech here)

From what you know of _______________, which parts of this position would be a perfect match and which parts might be a bit of a reach?

- There are two questions we have to ask in every reference call:
    - Do you have any knowledge of _______________________ ever being charged with a crime?
    - Are there any other people that you think we should talk to before deciding whether ____________________________ should work with youth?

Thank you for speaking with me. This has been a great help to our church.

Additional Questions for Reference Calls

- If we have the opportunity to hire youth ministry staff in addition to ____________, what kind of staff would complement him or her?
- Are there types of people or situations that ______________ works particularly well with or types of people or situations that are very difficult for him/her?
- Have you observed _______________ handle conflict situations of conflict? If yes, can you tell a little about the situation and how he or she handled it?
- Can you tell a little about your observations of his/her ability to manage others—staff or volunteers?
- What kinds of things motivate __________________? Do you have an example of a time that he/she was very enthusiastic?
- Have you ever heard ______________ express a desire for a resource that wasn't available in his/her previous position (such as supportive volunteers, a better youth budget, or something along those lines)?

PHONE AND/OR VIDEOCONFERENCE INTERVIEW QUESTIONS

APPENDIX M

Remember that these are the three main questions you want to answer in this interview:

1. Do I enjoy spending time with this person?
2. Does this person give every indication of being able to fulfill our job description?
3. Are this person's theology, style, and personality a fit our church?

As you prepare for the on-site interview, which should give you clear answers to the above three questions, the Search Team will want to select 10 must-ask questions from the list below or from an additional list of questions generated by your team.

The check boxes can help you narrow the list to the 10 most important for your church.

Leadership/Strategic Thinking

- ☐ Describe your involvement in shaping or influencing the direction of an organization you have served.
- ☐ Tell me about a time you helped a teenager through a tough situation.
- ☐ Describe your style and approach when you are leading large groups of students, calling teenagers you have not yet met, and leading small groups of students.
- ☐ How do you keep yourself organized on an ongoing basis?

- ☐ What was one of your best youth ministry experiences as a *leader*?
- ☐ What was one of your worst youth ministry experiences as a *leader*?
- ☐ How would you welcome strangers into youth group?
- ☐ What criteria would you use to evaluate the success of the programs our church currently has?
- ☐ Question specific to your church:

PROGRAM KNOWLEDGE/PASSION FOR YOUTH MINISTRY

- ☐ Describe your work you are doing now. How do you like it? *(Assessing satisfaction, optimism, whininess, energy level, and so on.)*
- ☐ Tell me about something that happened in your past youth ministry experience that really energized you.
- ☐ Tell me about something that happened in your past youth ministry experience that deflated your energy.
- ☐ Why do you want to be a youth minister?
- ☐ What do you see yourself doing in five years?
- ☐ Tell me a few success stories from your youth ministry.
- ☐ Question specific to your church:

MANAGEMENT STYLE

- ☐ Describe a time when you “sold” an idea under a particularly difficult circumstance.
- ☐ How do you create energy in your youth ministry?
- ☐ How would you describe your management style? Can you give examples of how your style has enhanced youth ministries you have managed?

- ☐ If I were to call a church/employer you used to work for, a current boss, or a fellow employee (because we might do that), what would they say about you? *(Looking for an answer that is honest, balanced. Are they confident enough to say something that is not necessarily flattering?)*

- ☐ How comfortable are you in front of parents?

PROBLEM SOLVING

- ☐ Tell about a conflict you've had in ministry and how it got resolved.

- ☐ Tell about a big mistake you've made in youth ministry or in your current job.

- ☐ Describe an experience where you worked with a staff member or volunteer who had some weak areas of performance. What tools did you use to bridge the gaps?

PERSONALITY/RELATIONAL

- ☐ What do you do for fun?

- ☐ What would you rather do: teach in front of a big group or lead a small group Bible study?

- ☐ What are some of your favorite youth ministry games?

- ☐ What was one of your best youth ministry experiences as a teenager?

- ☐ Heard any good jokes lately?

- ☐ If I looked at the front of your refrigerator, what would I see?

- ☐ What would I see if looked inside?

- ☐ What are the parts of a normal youth ministry job that you would give away if you could?

CONNECTING WITH TEENAGERS

- ☐ We know you enjoy all kinds of teenagers, or you wouldn't be in this business. But what kind of students do you enjoy working with the most?

- ☐ Why should teenagers who are not coming to church or to the youth group start to come? What are they missing? *(Looking for some idea about what the purpose of youth ministry is for the candidate.)*

- ☐ How would you reach out to students who are on the rolls but are not currently participating in our youth program? *(Looking for some idea about how creatively the candidate would pursue teenagers.)*

- ☐ Tell me about some good and bad experiences you've had with teenagers.

- ☐ What do you want students to know before they graduate from your youth group?

- ☐ (Pastoral Scenario) I'd like to know what you'd do in a situation like this. Suppose you see a student after church who is looking angry or sad. You say, "What's up?" The student says, "Well, nothing except I don't have any friends. I only had two anyway, but when I told them this week that they couldn't copy my homework anymore, they said they weren't my friends anymore. And they've been talking about me behind my back at school. So I'm basically friendless and a jerk. Other than that everything's great." How would you respond? *(Assessing pastoral sensitivity.)*

SPIRITUALITY

- ☐ Tell me what kind of a role God plays in your personal life. *(Listen for whether the vocabulary for faith experience is consistent with what the church would like to see communicated to its youth.)*
- ☐ How are you currently involved in your local church?
- ☐ Tell a little about your faith journey.
- ☐ Tell a little about your prayer life.
- ☐ Broad question: For you, what does it mean to be a Christian?
- ☐ How comfortable are you praying aloud in a group?
- ☐ What would you expect from the church where you serve?

DENOMINATION

- ☐ Why are you a *(denominational affiliation)?* Or why are you interested in serving in a *(denomination)* church?
- ☐ What role does the Bible have in your spiritual life?
- ☐ What role do the sacraments play in your spiritual life? *(If appropriate for your denomination.)*

OTHER

- ☐ What questions do you have for us? *(Interviewer: Be prepared to say, "I don't know, but I can find out.")*

INTERVIEW SCORECARD

APPENDIX N

The first column should include the skills identified by the committee and defined in the job description. Each church's criteria will be different. Candidates are scored on a scale of 1 to 10 with 1 being poor and 10 being excellent.

	Name	Name	Name	Name	Name	Name	Name	Name
Leadership/ Strategic Thinking	9	4						
Program Knowledge/Passion for Youth Ministry	10	6						
Management Style	10	6						
Problem Solving	9	5						
Personality/ Relational	9	6						
Connecting With Teenagers	10	7						
Spirituality	8	10						
Denominational/ Theological Fit	10	9						
Proven Success	10	6						
Other	9	10						
Total (100)	94	69						

JOB DESCRIPTION: HOST FOR ON-SITE INTERVIEW

APPENDIX O

Thank you for your willingness to serve as an on-site host for one of our top candidates for our church's open youth ministry position. You will serve as the candidate's guide and primary contact during the time this person is on site with us. On behalf of the search team, you will take on the following responsibilities:

- Contact the candidate and exchange contact information (e-mail addresses, cell numbers) and let the candidate know that you will be the host for his or her visit and that you'll be happy to answer any questions he or she might have.
- Ask your candidate whether he or she would prefer to stay in a hotel or with a family. Different people will have different preferences—and they're both OK—but for people-persons, sometimes the hospitality of a great family helps them say, "I belong here."
- In coordination with the Search Team chair, ensure that arrangements for transportation (flight and car), housing, and meals are made.
- Make arrangements to meet the candidate at an agreed-upon location (such as the airport or the church) at a specific time.
- Give the candidate a brief tour of the church and the community.
- Introduce the candidate to staff and any other individuals you run into during your time together.

- Ensure that the candidate has a copy of the schedule for his or her visit.
- Ensure that the candidate gets to where he or she needs to be on time.
- Answer questions the candidate may have. If you don't know the answers, offer to find out and get back to the candidate in a timely manner.
- At the end of the visit, thank the candidate for coming and offer to be available for any questions he or she may have after returning home.

If at any time you have questions about the candidate's schedule or need further information, contact ____________________________________ from the Search Team at ____________________________________.

TWO EXAMPLES OF ON-SITE SCHEDULES

APPENDIX P

Chapter 8 will help you understand the context of these sample schedules. It will also describe in more detail what might happen at each step.

We recommend that out-of-town visitors spend at least a full 24 hours visiting your church and community. Local candidates can be scheduled for a one-day visit.

Saturday and Sundays can be great days for on-site interviews, giving candidates a good feel for the church's worship style and for what the church is like during its most intense programming time. Each church, of course, will design its own unique schedule for an on-site interview, but we have included this sample to provide your search team with a starting point.

FOR A CANDIDATE COMING FROM OUT OF TOWN

Saturday

Afternoon—Candidate arrives and is met by host, meets the staff (since it is a Saturday, you'll want to prearrange times to meet key staff members in 30- to 60-minute blocks), and is given a tour of the church campus and the local area. Show off your church and community and their assets.

Purpose: This informal environment gives a candidate a nonthreatening opportunity to ease into the interview process, meet the staff, and become familiar with the face of the congregation. It also gives the host an opportunity to get to know the candidate on a personal level.

What to look for: Ease at which the candidate interacts with others, appropriateness in conversation, and whether the candidate is excited to be there.

6 p.m.—Dinner with candidate in informal setting with leaders and selected students at the home of a youth family; pastors are invited.

Purpose: To allow you and the candidate to experience each other in an informal large group setting, which is how the youth pastor will spend a lot of his or her time. It also allows church members and the candidate to get to know each other (helps both to judge if it's going to be a good fit). Never underestimate the relationship factor.

What to look for: The ease with which the candidate interacts in an informal large group setting. Does he or she participate in conversations with both teenagers and adults? Is the candidate engaging?

8 p.m.—Downtime for the candidate to rest up after a long day.

Sunday

Morning—Candidate attends worship services with host and attends one of the youth Sunday school classes.

Purpose: Gives the candidate a good snapshot of the church and teenagers in your natural environments. Gives another layer of teenagers' exposure to the candidate; it's good to get their input, and it helps determine the fit.

What to look for: Interaction with the people around him or her, level of comfort, encouraging words from the candidate.

12:30-3 p.m.—Lunch and interview with Search Team.

Purpose: To discern if God is calling this candidate to serve with you.

What to look for: A snapshot of the life of the candidate, level of transparency and honesty, known strengths and weaknesses, answers to issues you want to probe deeper, his or her approach to doing youth ministry. Do you enjoy being in the room with this person? Are you energized by the conversation?

3-5 p.m.—An afternoon excursion with a few students and adults to a place that showcases your community.

Purpose: To help the candidate imagine living in your town and partnering with the people of your church.

What to look for: Energy level, positive or negative outlook, level of interest in what your community offers. Did you enjoy the time you spent together?

5:30 p.m.—Candidate departs.

Or if you have a Sunday night youth program, the candidate might be able to attend, speak for a few minutes, and depart after the program.

ALTERNATIVE FOR LOCAL CANDIDATES (ONE-DAY INTERVIEW)

If the candidate is local, this can all be done in one full day; Sunday is recommended. If Saturday is a better day for one or both parties, encourage the candidate to come back and attend worship another Sunday.

Sunday

Morning—Candidate arrives and is met by host; attends worship services and a youth Sunday school class (introduced to students).

12/12:30-3 p.m.—Lunch and interview with Search Team.

3 p.m.—Host gives candidate tour of church and community.

5:30 p.m.—Dinner with candidate in informal setting with leaders and students at the home of a youth family; pastors are invited.

7:30 p.m.—Candidate departs.

SAMPLE JOB OFFER LETTER

APPENDIX Q

Dear __________________________________,

It is my pleasure to extend the following offer of employment to you on behalf of ______________________________ Church.

(Here you would insert one or two encouraging sentences, specific to this person's personality and gifts and express why you are thrilled to extend this offer to him or her.)

I am attaching your job description, but here are a few specific terms related to the offer that I want to make sure are clear:

Your title will be ______________________________________, and you will report to _______________________________.

Your annual salary will be $____________________, paid in bi-weekly installments of $__________________, subject to deductions for taxes and other withholdings as required by law or the policies of our congregation.

Your position will include the following benefits:

- 3 weeks' paid vacation
- 1-week study leave
- Health Benefits will be as follows: ____________________________

The church also plans to assist with the cost of your move, up to a total of $__________________.

The youth ministry budget will include a leadership expense line item of $_________________________ per year to cover any normal travel, phone, or other expenses occurred in the process of executing the responsibilities of your position.

We look forward to your beginning your first day with us on _____________
_________________________________.

(You will want to conclude with one more encouraging sentence that expresses enthusiasm about the new staff person joining your staff.)

Signature(s) of the clergy person and/or lay persons responsible for hiring and managing the youth director:

____

(For the Church: Name, Date)

____

(Candidate's Name, Date)

Include below the signature: This offer letter, along with the final form of any referenced documents, represents the entire agreement between the church and ________________________________, and no verbal or written agreements, promises, or representations that are not specifically stated in this offer, are or will be binding upon our church. If you are in agreement with the above outline, please sign. This offer will be in effect for five business days.

CHECKLIST FOR CREATING A MOMENTUM-BUILDING FIRST MONTH ON THE JOB

APPENDIX R

As you look toward welcoming your new youth pastor, we have created a master checklist to help the Welcoming Coordinator manage the many details of launching the new youth pastor well:

BEFORE THE FIRST DAY

- ☐ Make sure your youth pastor's new office or desk is ready to go and stocked with pencils, stapler, and other supplies. If he or she has a favorite candy bar or drink, slip a few into the desk drawer.
- ☐ Set up the e-mail address.
- ☐ If your church has a staff directory on the website, add your new youth pastor to it. If the page uses photos, see if your new youth pastor has a photo on file that you could use.
- ☐ Prepare an on-boarding packet, which will be given to your new hire on the first day of work. The packet typically includes:
    - W-4 to complete.
    - The church's employee manual. Highlight the parts that everyone wants to know but doesn't want to ask the boss about: sick days, holidays, vacations.
    - The church's visioning documents.
    - List of names and phone numbers of church staff and key church leaders. Many churches have this on their website and can simply print it out.

- A directory of contact information for all youth and their families.
- A calendar of any events that are currently scheduled in the youth ministry, as well as any major events on the church's calendar for the coming year.
- A directory of all church members; a photo directory would be ideal.
- A map of the city with key places highlighted.
- A city phone book.
- The church's employee handbook.
- Any inside information about office procedure (such as if there is a code to use for the copy machine and other important details).

MOVING DAY (IF THE YOUTH PASTOR IS MOVING FROM A DIFFERENT CITY)

- [ ] A great touch is to have youth, parents, and volunteers help unload the moving van into the youth pastor's new apartment or home.
- [ ] Another nice tradition in some churches is to "pound" the new staff member. The name comes from the idea that people in the congregation pre-stock the kitchen with a pound of sugar, a pound of butter, and so on. It's helpful do a little research ahead of time about the newcomer's favorite items, breakfast cereals, and whatnot.
- [ ] Arrange to have someone bring lunch or dinner over.

FIRST DAY ON THE JOB

When your new youth pastor goes home at the end of the first day, you want him or her to think, "Yes! I am so glad I am working at this church." The first day should feel like a celebration, not a chore.

- ☐ Schedule a welcome lunch with a friendly staff person or two.
- ☐ Offer a tour of the campus. You might have done this when the person was interviewing, but he or she will need it again. (Where did you say the copy machine is?)
- ☐ Orient the new staff person to "normal" office policies and processes. Consider little details like where to find office supplies, coffee machine etiquette, copy machine code, setting up voice mail and e-mail, times for required meetings, clarifying who does what on staff, how to fill out check request forms, facilities or vehicle request forms, and introduction to sound equipment.

THE FIRST FEW WEEKS

- ☐ **Meeting Families:** Implement a process that helps the new youth pastor meet as many families as possible, as quickly as possible. Some churches have receptions at church. Some choose a more time-consuming but more intimate process of scheduling a series of smaller dessert parties with 5 to 10 families at a time.
- ☐ **Becoming Acquainted With Staff:** Schedule a series of 30- to 60-minute meetings with key staff members, spread out over several days. The goal is to help the new staff member feel integrated into the team. Let them get to know each other as people. You can be creative: The meeting with the custodian can be a tour of the campus. Another staff member might want to take the youth pastor to a great local lunch spot. The meeting with the youth pastor's immediate supervisor should be within the first day or two.
- ☐ **Making Friends:** Try to introduce the youth pastor to peers, too. It's hard to make friends in a new town. In addition to middle school students and their parents, the youth pastor will need some other friends, too. If there isn't a large peer group in the church itself, guide the youth pastor to places where they can be found; nearby colleges, hobby groups, sports leagues, and other youth pastors are good places to start.
- ☐ **Supporting the Rest of the Family:** If the youth pastor is married, assign a "welcome buddy" to help the spouse get

acclimated. Be sensitive to how much or how little help and attention the newcomer would like. Lunches, tours of the town (best stores, great parks, and so on), and offers to help unpack are always appreciated, even if they are turned down.

CREATIVE IDEAS FOR WELCOMING A NEW YOUTH PASTOR

APPENDIX S

When a candidate agrees to accept the position, either the Search Team or a newly formed Welcome Committee can plan events and activities to welcome the new candidate and to ensure a smooth relocation. Here are a few ideas. Pick one or two to implement, but don't try to do them all.

- If the candidate has children, arrange for families and teenagers to assist with the children and childcare on moving day, as well as throughout the transition period.

- Ask the congregation to create a "welcome basket." Members of all ages can be asked to donate gift cards from their favorite restaurant or store, memberships for their favorite museum or park, or subscriptions to their favorite local newspaper or magazines.

- Ask members to create a page for a book entitled, "My perfect day in *(your town)*," which will include ideas for day trips in the area.

- Plan a special time during worship to introduce the candidate to the congregation. The opportunity might include a commissioning or some way for blessing the candidate's new ministry. After the service, plan a celebration to mark the candidate's arrival and start of ministry with your congregation.

- Plan multiple "Meet and Greet" opportunities for the candidate to quickly meet members of the congregation and for members of the church to have the chance to meet the new candidate. These can be arranged by neighborhoods, age groups (such as young adults, families with sixth-graders, high schoolers, middle-aged couples, octogenarians), or interest groups (such as mountain climbers, worship leaders, choir, Sunday School teachers, youth volunteers, parents).

- Create a three- to six-month calendar listing "strategic appearances" for a new staff person. Such items might include homecoming events at local high schools, town traditions (Powder Puff Football on Thanksgiving or the Tree Lighting), men's Bible study pancake breakfast, women's bake sale, Fourth of July parade, and so on.
- Clean (maybe even paint) the new youth pastor's office.
- Organize the youth closet.
- Create a photo album with pictures of each teenager or volunteer, with a list of three things the candidate will want to know about that person.
- If the new youth pastor is the playful type, some churches let their youth pull a low-key "welcome" prank. For example, the youth at one church bought two cases of root beer, the youth pastor's favorite drink, and placed the cans in various surprise hiding places: in drawers, closets, and bookshelves.

ACKNOWLEDGEMENTS

None of us is as smart as all of us.

- Ken Blanchard

This book was, in many ways, inspired by other people's stories, wisdom, and experiences. We're grateful for the privilege of being observers and partners with so many friends in youth ministry and specifically for the dozens of youth ministry rookies and veterans, clergy, and search teams whose experiences have found their way into these pages.

We want to thank first the youth and adult leaders of First Presbyterian Church in Nashville, Tennessee, and Christ United Methodist Church in Venice, Florida. The roller coaster ride of life together, the breath-stealing belly laughs, the unashamed sweat, and times the tears have flowed freely are a sweet reminder that someone greater than us is in charge—because we clearly are not.

The unique giftedness and passion of the youth staffs at First Presbyterian (Katy, Scott, Courtney, Teddy, Trey, Linda, Ryan, Ellie, and Erika) and Christ United Methodist (Susan, Marcia, Deanna, Sean, and Bekah) have shaped not only much of what is written in these pages but also who we are as well. Thanks for walking boldly into ambiguity every day.

We are grateful for that curious cohort of holy friends on our Youth Ministry Architects lead team (Betsy, Colyer, Dave, David, Jen, Lesleigh, Lynn, Sara, Stephanie), who have contributed to many of these ideas, tested others, and constantly find ways to make us better.

Our growing family of YMA churches has entrusted us with the awesome privilege of mentoring, befriending, and partnering in this mission to build sustainable youth ministries one church at a time. It was in your churches that so many ideas in this book were discovered and moved from vague theories to time-tested practices. We are grateful.

Thanks to our already busy friends who took time to read and improve these pages before they saw the light of day: Jules Postema, Andrew Suite, David Dunn-Rankin, Ben Kane, Jeff Wertz, Ann Bailey, Caroline Rossini, Becky

Ellenberger, and to our partners at Group and Simply Youth Ministry—Rick Lawrence, Doug Fields, Scott Firestone, Andy Brazelton, and Nadim Najm.

And now for a few personal words…

I (Mark) am particularly grateful for

- Jeff, for partnering with me in YMA's incremental revolution and for laughing louder than anyone else when I try to be funny
- My pastor, Todd Jones, and the elders and staff of First Presbyterian Church, who grant me much more freedom and honor than I deserve
- Chan Sheppard, my running buddy and treasured friend
- The pioneers at the Center for Youth Ministry Training—Deech, Lesleigh, Andrew, and Mindi—who are asking all the right questions about the training of indispensable youth pastors
- Adam, Sara, Debbie, Trey, and Leigh, who have long since moved from being our children to being our dearest friends and partners in the gospel
- My bride, Susan; you give me an unfair advantage.

I (Jeff) am especially grateful for my family, colleagues and coaches:

- Mark, no one could ask for a better trailblazer, leader and friend. Thanks for inviting me along.
- My pastor, Jerry, and people of Christ United Methodist for loving God and loving kids—and loving them in the right order. Thanks for taking a leap of faith for me long ago and continuing to bless my life.
- Fellow workers in the field: Larry, Al, Bob, Bobby, Cheryl, Dan, Dick, Edna Kate, Esther, Glenn, Jack, JoEllen, Ken, Kevin, Kyla, Lenee, Linda, Michele, Paul, Sandra, and my buddies at One Christ/Won City.
- The bosses who gave me room to fail forward and learn: Dad, Steve, Jim, Mark, Bob, Marsha, Dave, Buddy, and the guy at Milton's Pizza.
- My kind and wise family: Dad, Mom, Peter, David, Debbie, and Mike, whose insights are woven throughout these pages.
- Matthew and Katie—you are exactly what we dreamed of.
- Mary Lou—you are more.

And to the God who is the only indispensable one—who grants us both humility and value by allowing us to be minor characters in a major story.

THE PARABLE OF THE HOLEY MAN

A man falls into a deep hole and finds himself stuck—alone and in the dark. For a few anxious hours, he tries to jump or climb his way out, but the 20-foot walls are slippery and cold. It doesn't take long before he gives up and collapses in a dark corner.

Just when he thinks there's no way out, an old friend walks by the hole and peers over to see his buddy.

"Hey," he says, "I see you fell into a hole."

"Yes, I did," says the man. "I feel so helpless."

"Of course you do," says the friend at the top of the well. "You should be more careful. Even I could have told you this is what happens when you don't watch where you're going." He chuckles, then pauses for a moment. "Hey, just kidding buddy," he says. "I feel your pain. Listen, I'll be sure to pray for you. Stay warm." And he walks away.

A few tense hours later, another friend walks by. "Hey," she says, "I see you fell into a hole."

"Yes," says the man. "Can you help me?"

“Of course I can,” says the friend. “I fell into a hole once. In fact I have this great book about how to avoid holes in the future. Here—catch!” She tosses the book into the deep, dark hole. And she walks away.

Just about the time the man has abandoned all hope, a third friend comes by. “Hey,” he says, “I see you fell into a hole.”

“Yes,” says the man. “I don’t think I’ll ever get out.” “Scoot over,” says the third friend, and he climbs down into the hole. “Are you crazy?” says the man. “Now we’re both stuck down here!” “Don’t panic,” says his friend, “I’ve been in this hole before, and I know the way out.”